ANSWERING THE CALL
IN TIME OF WAR

A History of Camp Kohler
and the Western Signal Corps School

Danny M. Johnson

Johnson, Danny M.

Answering the Call in Time of War. A History of Camp Kohler and the Western Signal Corps School by Danny M. Johnson. Sacramento: I Street Press, 2018.

ISBN: 978-1-945526-48-0

1.Camp Kohler 2. Walerga 3. U.S. Army Posts

Library of Congress Control Number: 2018953371

Front cover design by Danny M. Johnson. Photo from *Radio News*, Special U.S Army Signal Corps Issue, vol. 31, no.5 (Chicago, IL, Feb. 1944).

Back cover design by Evelyn E. Di Salvo. Shoulder sleeve insignia courtesy of The U.S. Army Institute of Heraldry, Fort Belvoir. VA

Title page photo by Army Public Relations reprinted from *A Camera Trip through Camp Kohler*, (Brooklyn, New York,1943).

I Street Press
828 I Street
Sacramento, CA 95814

Additional copies may be obtained from Amazon.com

CONTENTS

ABOUT THE AUTHOR

Danny M. Johnson worked as a civilian on the Department of the Army staff at the Pentagon; as a Command Historian for the US Army Information Systems Command, Fort Huachuca, AZ; and as Chief of Public Affairs and Command Historian for HQ 5th Signal Command, Mannheim, Germany. In 2003, he traveled to Iraq to document the Signal Corps involvement in the US invasion. The Signal Corps Regimental Association awarded him the Bronze Order of Mercury before he retired as a Department of the Army civilian in October 2004 after 35 years of service. With 25 years of service in the Regular Army, Army National Guard, and Army Reserve, Johnson retired with the rank of Lieutenant Colonel in October 2006.

As a private military scholar, Danny M. Johnson has made numerous contributions *to On Point*, *The Journal of Army History*, and numerous other professional military historical publications. He specializes in World War II; Old Posts, Camps and Stations; unit history; and Army heraldic insignia, some of which he helped to design. He has authored *Military Communications Supporting Peacekeeping Operations in the Balkans* (2000) and edited *The European Signal Corps Order of Battle* (2001). He has also contributed numerous inserts to *The Oxford Companion to Military History* (2001), the *Army Lineage Series* book*, Signal Corps (2005), and Military Communications from Ancient Times to the 21st Century* (2007). He currently resides in Sacramento, California.

DEDICATION

In our fight against the forces of evil, the changeability and diversity of battlefronts across the globe, together with the scope of the struggle, placed a greater emphasis on fighting the battle of communications in World War II than in any other war in our history. Thousands of trained signal soldiers who could function proficiently and promptly in the heat of battle were a criterion for victory. To this end, I dedicate this book to the soldiers of Camp Kohler and the Western Signal Corps School at Davis and to the United States Army Signal Corps.

ACKNOWLEDGEMENTS

I wish to recognize certain organizations who provided their time and resources to help make this book a reality. The Sacramento County Recorder's Office provided vital detailed information on land records for the Camp Kohler area, and the personnel in the Sacramento Room of the Sacramento Main Library encouraged me to write this definitive history of Camp Kohler. I also wish to thank SGM (CA) Dan Sebby, California State Military Reserve, for all the documents related to Camp Kohler that are made available through the California State Military Museum website, http://militarymuseum.org/.

I give special thanks to Gerry Ward from the I Street Press for all his technical knowledge in the preparation of this book. He was a big help to me!

I especially wish to recognize the outstanding editorial support from my wife, Beverly, who reworked numerous versions of the manuscript before it ever became a book. Her understanding, support, encouragement, and suggestions of what had to be done to achieve an outstanding product will not be forgotten. I must also thank my wife for her patience, and professionalism during the constant rewriting of this manuscript.

BEGINNINGS

What do a migrant worker camp, a Japanese American assembly center, an Army Signal Corps training center, a prisoner of war branch camp, an Army Air Corps overseas replacement depot, an Army branch port of embarkation, and Walerga engineer depot have in common? They were all located on the same property as Camp Kohler, California. The Army land holdings in Sacramento County would grow from a 160-acre tract in 1942 to over some 3,800 acres at its high point in 1944. Most of the land was leased throughout its history and returned to its owners starting in 1946 when no longer needed by the Army.

SACRAMENTO ASSEMBLY CENTER

On acreage originally belonging to the Rancho Del Paso land grant located twelve miles northeast of the city of Sacramento, Camp Kohler was one of fifteen temporary detention sites known as "assembly centers" and run by the Wartime Civil Control Administration (WCCA).[1] The Sacramento assembly center, often called Walerga after a railroad flag station near the locality, housed 4,739 Japanese Americans who had been removed from Sacramento and San Joaquin counties during the spring of 1942. They were housed at the assembly center while they waited to be transferred to a more permanent War Relocation Authority (WRA) camp at Tule Lake, Modoc County, California. Walerga was one of the smaller WCCA camps and operated for only 52 days, from 6 May to 26 June 1942.

The War Department leased the land for Walerga through eminent domain from the owners, Mr. Dean Dillman and his sister, Mrs. Corinne Dillman Kirchofer. (See complete list of leases in Appendix A.) The camp, built to house 5,000 Japanese Americans, was located on a 160-acre tract in the center of an oak grove in a rural

1

location northeast of Sacramento where according to Lt. Gen. John L. DeWitt, commanding general of the Western Defense Command and Fourth Army, "a migrant camp had once operated, and advantage was taken of nearby utilities. However, construction was substantially all new there."[2]

Lt. Gen. DeWitt, personnel from his staff, and the

Aerial view of Sacramento Assembly Center, California. Courtesy of National Archives, 1942

staff of the WCCA inspected the newly completed Walerga assembly center on 1 May 1942.[3] All structures in the camp were placed in five functionally organized city blocks, laid out by the Corps of Engineers and built by private contractors. "Aerial photographs indicate there were 11 blocks with over 225 tar paper-covered buildings."[4] Theater of Operations type buildings, better known as T/O buildings, were used by the Corps of Engineers in assembly center construction.[5] Evacuee barracks were of a modified T/O design resulting in temporary buildings that were inexpensive, avoided the use of critical war materials, and could be assembled

2

quickly. Approximately 200 of these buildings were barracks typically built for these centers. Each barrack was 100 by 20 feet, single story, and divided into five 20 by 20-foot apartments that would accommodate from ten to twelve persons apiece. Normally, housing blocks were engineered for a capacity of 1,000 persons, to be served by two community kitchens and mess halls.

> "Walerga, a cluster of wooden shacks, was palatial compared to other California assembly centers," said Sacramento State [University] archivist Julie Thomas. "Most of the centers were at fairgrounds or racetracks, and families of six were forced to live in stables they had to clear out themselves."[6]

Landscaping of Camp Kohler. Photo by PFC Aaron Appelson, *Message* Staff. Reprinted from *Camp Kohler Message,* (Camp Kohler, CA, 14 January 1943) p. 4.

Within each block, showers, lavatories, and toilet facilities were erected. The camp had its own three-building 150-bed infirmary, setup and operated by a

Japanese American medical staff. Laundries, canteens, post offices, a bank, dental clinics, barber shops, warehouses, recreation buildings, administration buildings and places for the reception of visitors had to be built. Housing for military police was provided in an area separate from the assembly center enclosure.

A newly arrived family being escorted by a volunteer guide to their assigned location in the barracks, Sacramento Assembly Center, California. Photo by Dorothea Lange, 20 May 1942, Courtesy of *Densho Encyclopedia* (17 July 2015). Retrieved 15:59, 12 August 2017 from http://encyclopedia.densho.org/sources/en-dron Aaenshopd-i151-00027-1.

Mr. Roy C. Donnally, manager of the Sacramento office of the United States Employment Service oversaw registering and evacuation of Japanese Americans from the Sacramento area to Walerga.[7] Mr. Gene Kenyon, district manager of the Works Projects Administration (WPA) and his staff oversaw the camp administration at Camp Walerga.[8]

The initial group of several hundred volunteer Japanese Americans first arrived at Walerga on 6 May 1942. They were the lead element of an advance party helping to prepare the camp for arrival of Sacramento's entire 3,500 population of Japanese Americans mandated to arrive at Walerga by not later than 16 May 1942. According to WPA officials, the Japanese Americans had their own form of self-government within the camp. They elected their own council members for democratic representation within their own housing blocks at Walerga, and it likely carried forward to the more permanent relocation camp at Tule Lake.[9] At the high point of its operation on 30 May 1942 the Sacramento assembly center housed 4,739 evacuated Japanese Americans.[10]

The first contingent of almost 500 of Sacramento's approximately 5,000 evacuated Japanese Americans departed the Walerga rail siding on 15 June 1942 by overnight train from the assembly center, arriving at Tule Lake relocation center, Modoc County, California, the next morning. "This initial transfer represents the first major movement inland of Japanese evacuated from West Coast military areas," the Sacramento Bee reported.[11] For the next nine days, almost 500 evacuees per day were transferred to Tule Lake by train. Some 85 center evacuees stayed behind to clean up Walerga prior to its closing.

The WCCA had earlier reported on 20 June 1942 that once the camp closed on or about 26 June 1942 that "some other government agency probably will move into the Walerga assembly center after the last evacuated Japanese leave there 24 June."[12] The WCCA spokesman went on to say, "The representatives of a number of federal agencies have been looking the camp over during the past several days."[13] The last 85 Japanese Americans were transferred to Tule Lake on 26 June 1942. The same day, the WCCA closed the center making it available for the War Department to assume control of the facility on 8 July 1942. The Sacramento assembly center had cost the Corps of Engineers and the WPA $821,682.00 and $56,660.00 respectively.[14]

The War Department's interest in the camp had begun in early June 1942 because the Signal Corps had a training limit of around 20,000 soldiers at its two training centers—14,000 at Camp Crowder, Missouri and 6,000 at Fort Monmouth, New Jersey. The Signal Corps regularly taught courses lasting from 6 weeks up to 13 weeks, so it calculated that it should deliver somewhere in the range of 58,000 technicians at the two training centers before the year's end. However, that figure still fell 12,000 below the mark of meeting the Army's computed requirements for 70,000 signalmen. There was no physical space for further growth at the Fort Monmouth center, and any further development at Camp Crowder would first necessitate additional construction, so Camp Kohler became the third replacement training center.[15]

The Walerga assembly center had all the characteristics of being the most suitable site available. It had space for 5,000 soldiers, and it could be made available, having been abandoned recently by the inland movement of Japanese American internees. It apparently met General Olmstead's specifics for a training center on the West Coast, and it could be made ready to receive trainees inside of a month. On 2 July 1942 the War Department approved its acquisition, forewarning the Signal Corps that the proposed focus would be just a temporary solution. It was possible that it would be closed by 31 December 1942.[16] However, the camp remained open, and growth continued between 1942 and 1946. The Sacramento assembly center property which had become Camp Kohler would eventually consist of 17 leases obtained through federal eminent domain proceedings along with a few state and county easements to include sewer and a railroad right of way. (Refer to Appendix A: Camp Kohler Real Property Leases.)

The Signal Corps took ownership of the camp on 8 July 1942, and the Ninth Service Command activated Camp Kohler on 28 July 1942. Col. John R. Young assumed command of the station complement, Service Command Unit (SCU) No.1933. (Refer to definition of SCU.)[17] On 20 August in Washington, DC, Robert P. Patterson, undersecretary of war, announced that a new Signal Corps replacement training center would be opened about 15 September at Walerga and would be called Camp Kohler[18] with BG. Stephen H. Sherrill as commander. Sherrill had recently served in Washington, DC, in the office of the chief of signal and earlier with the operations division of the war department general staff. After being promoted on 18 August, Brigadier General Sherrill arrived at Camp Kohler on 28 August and took command on 1 September with Col. William S. Morris serving as director of training.[19] Camp Kohler was established on 1 September 1942 as the third Signal Corps replacement training center under the jurisdiction of the Ninth Service Command, Fort Douglas, Utah, in order to help meet the ever-increasing need for trained specialists to operate and maintain the Army's vast communications system in a war which already had become global in its proportions.

1LT. FREDERICK L. KOHLER

1st **Lt. Frederick L. Kohler.** Reprinted from *Camp Kohler Message*, (Camp Kohler, CA, 26 November 1942), p.1.

Camp Kohler was named in honor of 1Lt. Frederick L. Kohler, a young Signal Corps officer from Oakland, California. He was a 1940 electrical engineering graduate of the University of California, Berkeley, who lost his life on 14 March 1942 while with the Chinese military mission of Army LtG. Joseph W. Stillwell.

Kohler was a passenger on a China National Aviation Corporation (CNAC) airliner bound for Chungking, China when the aircraft, the last CNAC Douglas DC-2-221 #31 (named Chungshan), developed mechanical trouble just after takeoff from Kunming, China, and crashed into a hillside just four miles from the airport. The plane was reported to have burst into flames in midair. The tail of the plane was reported to have been ripped off during the crash. The probable cause of the crash was due to engine failure, a soft wet airfield, and overloading.[20]

Four survivors of the crash dragged out as many of the passengers as they could before flames spread throughout the wreckage. In all, thirteen passengers were killed in the crash with five Americans, including Kohler, amongst the dead. The Americans killed in the crash were buried on 16 March 1942 at the Chinese Army Air Force cemetery four miles outside of Kunming. BG. Claire L. Chennault, head of the American volunteer group (AVG) better known as the "Flying Tigers" and other members of the AVG attended the service. Kohler was posthumously awarded the Paoting Medal of the Sixth Order by the Republic of China "in recognition of the exemplary services he rendered in helping the war effort of the United Nations and participating in Japanese aggression."[21] Kohler's remains were reinterred at Golden Gate National Cemetery, San Bruno, California, on 1 April 1949. He is buried in Section K, Site 179.[22]

READYING CAMP KOHLER

The proposal for rapidly getting 5,000 men into training at Camp Kohler did not work out as planned. It soon was evident that although there was housing for that number, the sanitary and medical facility support were sufficient for only 2,000 soldiers; therefore, the underlying limit was set at 2000, pending the extra development which would be required to make it equivalent to other training centers. Camp Kohler would confine training to the basic courses and send the qualified men on to Camp Crowder for specialized training. So far, there were no provisions at Camp Kohler for a target range, obstacle course, parade ground or gas chamber to offer reality to basic soldiers' training, and unlike Fort Monmouth, which was near a populated area, the new camp was situated in a rural area.[23] The *Sacramento Bee* reports the following in an article about the 45th reunion of the opening of Camp Kohler:

> Bob Crist, then a young lieutenant from Philadelphia, had his first view of Camp Kohler in August 1942, a few weeks before it officially opened. "I couldn't believe what I saw," Crist, 71, recalled recently. "They told me this was to be the 3rd Signal Corps Replacement Training Center in the States. I'd seen Fort Monmouth

9

and I knew about Camp Crowder. Now those were Signal Corps training centers.

"What I was looking at from the window of a bus was a collection of tar paper-covered buildings plopped together on a small hill. Someone mentioned we were about 12 miles from the city limits of Sacramento, in an area called Walerga."[24]

The main post area, eventually consisting of 805 acres, was used for troop messing, officer quarters and enlisted barracks, health care, and other soldier support functions found at most posts, camps, and stations. "The area contained 517 numbered structures, including 300 barracks buildings, a recreation hall, swimming pool, officers club, 330-bed hospital, five small obstacle courses. . . and a fire station. . .. The former Camp Kohler barracks were predominately constructed of wooden frames and tar paper, but soldiers eventually covered some with wooden shingles."[25] Mr. Andrew Smith of Roseville, California, who performed maintenance work at the camp, "recalls that the structures were intended to be wooden frames covered with canvas, but were covered with tar paper instead."[26] Most veterans who served at Kohler said the barracks were "flimsy, hot in the summer, cold in the winter, and very bare bones."[27] "According to 1943 and 1944 health and welfare reports, garbage from the barracks and mess halls was hauled to local farms to feed hogs, and the pit latrines were used in the barracks areas. Some combustible waste was burned on site."[28] The barracks had electricity supplied, but no sign of any transformer sites was identified. The areas around barracks were sparse with some street paving or landscaping present.

The initial 481 trainees arrived on 19 September 1942; basic training started two days later.[29] Cadres for Camp Kohler were officers and noncommissioned officers that originated from Fort Monmouth, New Jersey, and Camp Crowder, Missouri. As the only Signal Corps training center on the West Coast, Camp Kohler provided "a four weeks [sic] basic training course for inductees and enlisted men."[30] Basic Signal Corps training at Kohler included "the installation, maintenance, and operation of radio, telephone, telegraph, and teletype equipment used on permanent military installations within the country and by fighting units"[31] all over the world.

By 1 October 1942 there were 3,000 trainees, more than 50 percent over the limit initially approved. Now that Camp Kohler had been procured, the Signal Corps had no desire to surrender the site toward the end of the year. With the requirements for fully trained signalmen steadily mounting, the main expectation of holding Kohler in 1943 lay in changing over into a unit training center. Accordingly, plans for such a center with a limit of 5,700 trainees went ahead simultaneously with arrangements for Kohler's utilization as the third replacement training center.[32]

The War Department officially designated Camp Kohler with War Department General Order #54, dated 14 October 1942 for the late 1Lt. Frederick L. Kohler.[33] The installation was officially dedicated on 1 December 1942. Among those present to play a leading role in the dedication were the Army's chief signal officer, MG. Dawson Olmstead and BG. Stephen H. Sherrill, commanding general of the Western Signal Corps replacement training center (WSCRTC). In addition, LtC. Clay Anderson, Sacramento district Corps of Engineers representing Col. R. C. Hunter, Corps of Engineers, turned over the keys to the installation to Col. John R. Young, post commander.[34] Congressman Elect Leroy Johnson, third congressional district, also attended. Furthermore, Mr. and Mrs. Henry H. Kohler of Oakland, California, the parents of the late 1Lt. Frederick L. Kohler, were honored at the ceremony.[35] Because the official dedication ceremony for Camp Kohler had been closed to the public, KFBK radio in Sacramento broadcasted the ceremony on the evening of 2 December 1942.[36] Camp Kohler grew rapidly into a modern military training center, transforming hundreds of newly-inducted men into competent soldiers. The camp as an Army post, however, had a long way to go as there were inadequate post and training facilities. More had to be constructed even though contractors had been working on adding new buildings since July 1942. Frank Maloney, owner of a Sacramento firm, was one of many people to receive a government contract to build temporary frame buildings.[37]

Oak Grove Theater. Reprinted from *The Western Signal Corps Message*, (Camp Kohler, CA, 2 September 1943) p.6.

Nevertheless, until new buildings could be constructed, soldiers employed some imagination. For example, by using a former hospital tent, soldiers erected a new tent theater with a seating capacity for 400 persons in lieu of an unfinished post theater. In order not to obstruct the view on the inside of the tent, they put the supporting poles on the outside of the canvas covering. 1Lt. R. F. Coyle, post special service and theater officer, oversaw getting the tent erected. The canvas tent was near the

Tent Theater. Reprinted from *The Western Signal Corps Message,* (Camp Kohler, CA, 2 September 1943), p.6.

main gate and was also used for religious services.[38] The first services had previously been held in an oak grove under the open sky; later they were scattered in basic school buildings. Finally, the new chapel was finished and dedicated on 29 November 1942. The main auditorium could seat 360 persons and held offices for Camp Kohler's four chaplains. Each could convert the altar to suit his individual needs. In addition, the Army built a large choir loft in the back of the auditorium and equipped it with a new organ.[39]

The Post Chapel. Photo by Public Relations Office, Camp Kohler, CA., *A Camera Trip Through Camp Kohler* (Brooklyn, NY, August 1943)

Buildings went up quickly. By December 1942 there were a new 29-building station hospital unit, a camp recreational hall, officers' billets, two battalion recreational halls, a large chapel, and hundreds of barracks for trainees.[40] The new hospital opened in mid-December 1942 with LtC. Jacob L. Pritchard serving as chief surgeon and 1Lt. Mabel Stevens as chief nurse. Stevens was a veteran of the Bataan campaign in the Philippine Islands.[41]

The Station Hospital. Photo by Public Relations Office, Camp Kohler, CA. Reprinted in *A Camera Trip Through Camp Kohler* (Brooklyn, NY, August 1943)

The largest recreation hall contained a theater, gymnasium, canteen, and cafeteria.[42] Also, the camp and the replacement training center each occupied one of the two new headquarters buildings and nearly all the streets at the camp were paved.

In January 1943, Camp Kohler opened a guest house for visitors on Fort Monmouth Avenue. Visitors could rent rooms for 50 cents per person.[43] Also, during the summer of 1943, Camp Kohler set about upgrading the theater by adding a large air conditioning unit. Another remodel of the theater in late December 1943 added modern opera seats. "The purchase of the individual seats was made possible by funds obtained from ticket sales to service men," according to the *Sacramento Bee*.[44]

Camp Kohler Guest House. Photo by Public Relations Office, Camp Kohler, CA reprinted from *A Camera Trip Through Camp Kohler*. (Brooklyn NY, August 1943)

In 17 May 1943 Camp Kohler celebrated the grand opening of its brand new, five-acre, $700,000 laundry. The facility, constructed under the direction of the Army Corps of Engineers, employed 286 personnel. Starting wages at the time were a whopping 74 cents per hour. German prisoners of war at Camp Kohler augmented the civilian workforce in the laundry when needed as not all prisoners worked in agriculture. The laundry provided services for McClellan Field, Mather Field, Camp Kohler, and Western Signal Corps School in Davis, California.

The Post Theater. Photo by Public Relations Office, Camp Kohler, CA. Reprinted in *A Camera Trip through Camp Kohler,* (Brooklyn, NY, August 1943)

Camp Kohler/McClellan AFB Laundry. Photo by Army Corps of Engineers. Reprinted from *Former Utilized Defense Sites (FUDS),* (Sacramento District. Sacramento, CA, n.d.)

A look at the 1945 Camp Kohler Layout Plan reveals other important features of the Camp Kohler property. The camp water tower was located at the intersection of Allen Street and Evans Road. "The tank [had] a wooden structure supported by many large timbers. It had an inside diameter of 42.6 feet, a capacity of 125,000 gallons and was 128 feet high." Another feature of the camp was the parade ground, the southwest corner of which is described as the "oiled and graveled area." It lay 73.46 acres directly west of the base

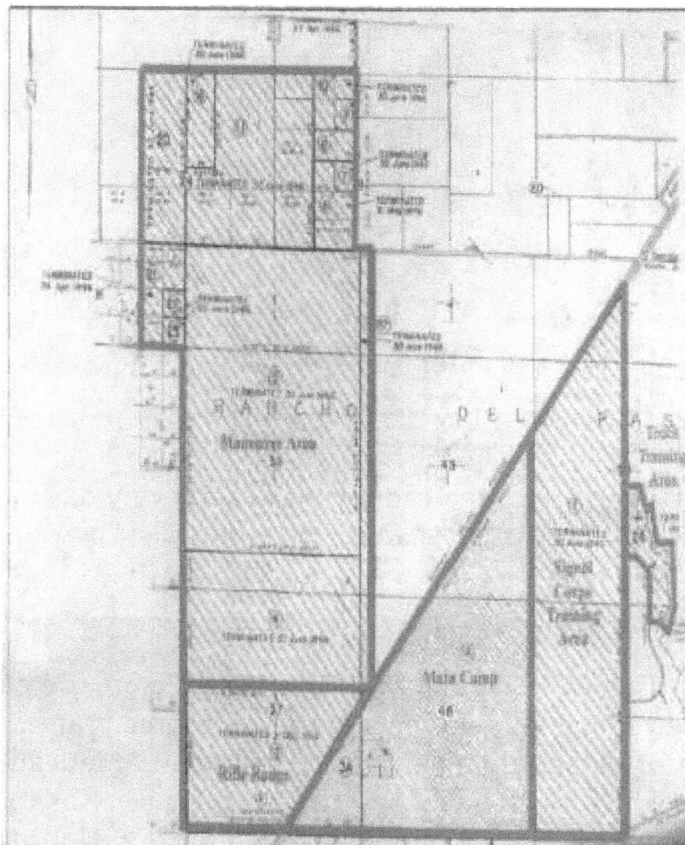

Camp Kohler Layout Plan. *Historic Posts, Camps, Stations, and Airfields,* http://www.military museum.org/CpKohler.html p3-14. (See Appendix F.)

hospital. Furthermore, the 1945 Camp Kohler Layout Plan shows a concrete slab motor pool with gas pumps, wash racks, and a grease rack. The motor pool serviced trucks used primarily in the truck driving course.[45]

Finally, Camp Kohler had its very own cannon for ceremonial activities. Trainees were detailed to clean the big gun, using a ramrod to clean the bore. They had to make it "spic and span" for inspection. They fired the cannon, which used blank ammunition, for the first time

This Goes Boom Every Day Photo reprinted from *The Western Signal Corps Message*, (Camp Kohler, CA, 24 August 1944) p. 5

on 1 January1943, the cannon was used every day at reveille and retreat after which a loudspeaker played recorded music.

SIGNAL CORPS ADDS HISTORIC STREET NAMES

The leadership of the WSCRTC at Camp Kohler decided to name the streets in the cantonment area in honor of outstanding heroes and events in American military history. Some of the street names were as follows: Avenue of the United Nations, named for the joint nation effort against the axis powers; Fort Monmouth Avenue, named for the Eastern Signal Corps Training Center; Camp Crowder Avenue, named for the Central Signal Corps Training Center; Bataan Street, named for a battle fought

7 January – 9 April 1942 which represented the most intense phase of Imperial Japan's invasion of the Philippines during World War II; Midway Street, named for a decisive naval battle in the Pacific Theater of World War II between 4 and 7 June 1942; Corregidor Street, named for the site of a costly siege and pitched battle between the Imperial Japanese Army and the U.S. Army during the first months of 1942; Dutch Harbor Street, named for a harbor on Amaknak Island in Unalaska, Alaska, when the Imperial Japanese Navy launched two aircraft carrier raids in June 1942; Colonel Murphy Street, named for a pioneer in the development of radio beams and equipment for military aircraft; Capt. Colin Kelly Street, named after one of the first American heroes of the war to sacrifice his own life to save his crew when his plane became the first American B-17 to be shot down in combat; Lt. Nininger Street, named for a platoon leader in the 57th Infantry (Philippine Scouts), who sacrificed his life on 12 January 1942 amid fierce fighting in Bataan and was posthumously awarded the Medal of Honor; Colonel Coles Street, named for the distinguished executive officer for the chief signal officer, AEF, WWI; Meyer Street, named for a brigadier general, Army signal expert, and first chief signal officer during and after the Civil War; and Chapel Grove, the location of the first outdoor church in a grove of oaks at Camp Kohler.[46]

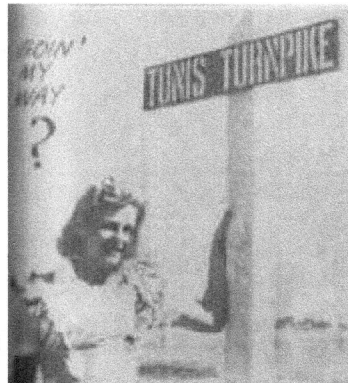

No Hitch Hiker, This Lassie. Photo reprinted from *The Western Signal Corps Message*, (Camp Kohler, CA,15 July 1943) p.1

By July 1943, additional street names were added. These names commemorated allied victories in World War II as well as

19

important Army heroes: Kohler Avenue for the young lieutenant who gave his life for his country; Mason Avenue for Captain Dale Mason, a signal officer who froze to death in Alaska; Allen Street for BG. James Allen who served as chief signal officer around 1910; Evans Road for LtC. Evans, signal officer of the Panama Canal Department; Gorgas Street for the former surgeon who helped in fighting malaria; and Sternberg Street for the surgeon general during the Spanish American War. In addition, three streets were renamed: Guadalcanal Street in honor of the famous battle in the Pacific, and Tunis Turnpike and Attu Road for important US victories. At this time, it was also decided that all roads running north and south would be considered avenues, and those running east and west would be considered streets.

SIGNAL CORPS REPLACEMENT TRAINING CENTER

Signal Corps replacement training centers were organized to have one or more training battalions. One of the primary missions was to train brand new recruits in the basic soldier skills. Soldiers were taught drill and ceremonies. They were also taught how to care for themselves and their personal belongings.

Tent Pitching and Instruction. Photo by Public Relations Office, Camp Kohler, CA. Reprinted from *A Camera Trip Through Camp Kohler*. (Brooklyn, NY, August 1943).

Signal Corps soldiers were trained to perform maintenance and operation of their equipment and serve as a trained combatant. They were thoroughly trained to use their weapons, and learned camouflage, scouting, patrol, map and aerial photograph reading, and how to protect themselves and their equipment from gas, air and mechanized attack. When teaching basic signal skills, instructors used a vocational approach. Students applied core signal principles and methods to the equipment to which they would be assigned. Trainees were rated by their instructors on each training module, as well as on military bearing and neatness, attention for duty, tact, conduct, initiative, intelligence, and dependability.

TRAINING ACTIVITIES

Some training required sizeable acreage, not only for the size of the equipment, but also to provide safety for the men. For example, areas with camouflage were needed for truck driver training and field exercises, and areas where soldiers used their weapons needed to be away from the main post. A description of some of these areas follows.

Motor Maintenance. Photo by Public Relations Office, Camp Kohler, CA. Reprinted from *A Camera Trip Through Camp Kohler*. (Brooklyn, NY, August 1943).

Truck Driver Training

Camp Kohler had its own motor transport school. The types of subjects covered in this sixteen-week course were engine shop work, chassis shop work, driving and maintaining all types of Army vehicles, and use of machine guns on trucks. Students also learned to drive trucks from the Camp Kohler motor pool to transport supplies and personnel both on and off post. Graduates from this school qualified as expert drivers and had the proper knowledge in the operation and maintenance of Army vehicles, rules of the road, and safety regulations. The motor transport school also trained women in the post administration functions as drivers of Army vehicles.

The Camp Kohler Motor Park. Photo by Public Relations Office, Camp Kohler, CA. Reprinted from *A Camera Trip Through Camp Kohler.* Brooklyn, NY, (August 1943).

Obstacle Courses

Camp Kohler had its own sizeable obstacle course designed and built by the post engineers in October 1942. The obstacle course was built west of the parade ground near Brett Drive in present day North Highlands. The 450-yard course contained a rope climb, fire trench, eight-foot divider, level stepping stool, rope swing, and tunnel crawl. Soldiers were required to run the course once per week.

Horizontal Ladder. Photo by Public Relations Office, Camp Kohler, CA. Reprinted from *A Camera Trip Through Camp Kohler. (Brooklyn, NY, August 1943)*

Rope Swing. Photo by Public Relations Office, Camp Kohler, CA. Reprinted from *A Camera Trip Through Camp Kohler.* (Brooklyn, NY, August 1943).

There was competition between the training companies and noteworthy competition between different bases in the region. Camp Kohler and Camp Beale close to Marysville maintained a fierce rivalry. At least five additional smaller obstacle courses with pits and climbing mechanical assembly were situated close to exercise areas that were near the barracks.

Rifle Range

Dry Practice in Rifle Marksmanship. Photo by Public Relations Office, Camp Kohler, CA. Reprinted in *A Trip through Camp Kohler (Brooklyn, NY, 1943).*

For the first few months, trainees had to travel to Camp Beale, California, to qualify in marksmanship. Finally, in November 1942, a new rifle range was built at Camp Kohler, west of the railroad tracks and away from the cantonment area. It took only twenty-three days. The 285-acre range, free of most structures, was 1000 feet long and had a 7-8-foot-high back wall. At least 20 infantry officers came from Fort Benning, Georgia, to teach basic weapon skills. "On the new range, up to 100 soldiers at a time could fire from 100, 200, and 300 feet."[47] When the range opened, the camp was honored to invite 1Sgt. Thomas N. Johns, a member of the Florida National Guard team which had won the Camp Perry matches in 1937 and 1938, to fire the first shot. Markedly, he split the bull's eye.[48] Because many of the soldiers had not had any experience using a weapon, the rifle range was open day and night. In 1987, the *Sacramento Bee* reported retired Col. John A. Joseph

24

as saying that it had been his job to "train those boys and feed them into combat as fast as possible."[49]

Communication Training under Battle Conditions

In 1943 the WSCRTC "acquired an additional 2 leased parcels totaling 697.04 acres"[50] where soldiers could practice their newly learned skills under real life conditions. The training center used the area for field exercises in telephone pole construction, stringing of exercises in telephone pole construction, stringing of communications lines, and truck driving practice.

Laying Temporary Wire Lines. Reprinted from *Western Signal Corps Message (Camp Kohler, CA, 15 July 1943) p.5.*

The 1945 Layout depicts 24 small, temporary structures in the training area, including storage sheds and a field kitchen. "The area was used to practice construction and operation of communications systems under field conditions and driving trucks on unimproved trails and rough terrain."[51]

When students became comfortable with their new skills, they advanced to field exercises under simulated battle conditions in the Tahoe National Forest near Sierra City, Sierra County, California. The first convoy of trucks and 250 soldiers went to the Tahoe National Forest on 24 May 1943 to practice all types of communications and maintenance learned during their specialist training. These training exercises lasted for five-day periods and were held in an area of approximately 20 square miles in that locality.[52]

Wire Crew Draws a Vital Thread for Important Communications between Two Units of Troops during Exercises in the Tahoe National Forest, CA. (U.S. Army Signal Corps Photo, reprinted in *Radio News, Special U.S. Army Signal Corps Issue,* Vol. 31, No. 5. (Chicago, Il., Feb.1944) p. 103.

Field Telephones Permit Privacy in Territory Where Enemy Troops Might Pick Up Signals from Radio Equipment. U.S. Army Signal Corps Photo, *Radio News, Special U.S Army Signal Corps Issue,* Vol. 31, No. 5, (Chicago, Il, Feb. 1944) p. 101.

Street Fighting

In September 1943 combat training soon took on a fast-moving tempo for Kohler soldiers with the initiation of a street-fighting tactical problem in a replicated French village. Four complete two-story buildings at a street corner were included, with roofless extensions on either end. Buildings were 18 feet wide, flanking one 50-foot street and crossroad 30 feet wide. The buildings extended for 75 yards. The barebones village was built near the then recently opened infiltration course. The *Sacramento Bee* reported, "Built under the supervision of Maj. A. S. Daley, chief of the small arms branch, the village will be used by the training division to emphasize hand to hand combat in the step to step capture of an enemy occupied position."[53] Almost any type of situation encountered in combat at close quarters could be set up in the village area. Emphasis was placed on protection from booby traps currently being used extensively by the enemy.

Explosion on Infiltration Course. Reprinted from *The Western Signal Corps Message* (Camp Kohler, CA, August 1943). p. 26

Village Combat Fighting. Reprinted from *The Western Signal Corps Message*, (Camp Kohler, CA, 2 December 1943) p. 5

Approaching the village from the south, troops encountered wire, fortifications, and obstacles while under blank fire from the entrenched "enemy" as well as surprise targets at varying distances. Firing blank ammunition, the advancing troops executed the prescribed problem. Double-apron barbed wire complicated the entrance to the village, and a machine gun was in operation against the men as they advanced.

Each building contained furniture, with numerous booby traps concealed in typical places. Battle confusion in sound, sight, and odor were provided with various props including water, gas, flour, and smoke.

Landing Net Training

An adapted debarkation platform, mimicking the side of a troop transport, furnished Camp Kohler men with familiarity in going over the side of a ship and down a rope net. Erected in the obstacle course vicinity, the new training apparatus had been incorporated into the normal physical fitness program, and all training and administrative organizations were required to work out on the net every other week amongst the reserved obstacle course sessions. "The debarkation scaffold is not an ordered feature of training but was added by the training division upon suggestion from other camps, where it has met with much success."[54]

"The scaffold is comparable to a transport, although not the exact size. The deck is 26 feet, above the ground, with a four-foot deck rail around the 13 X 25-foot deck. A stairway leads to the top of the scaffold."[55] The manila rope landing nets were woven into a rectangular design so that the men had a place to support their feet on the way down. Heavy weights held the net in place. After the first men got down, they wiggled the net to represent the motion of getting onto a small landing craft. All men were taught a uniform strategy for avoiding collisions with other soldiers or having their hands stepped on. They all moved their arms and legs in a synchronized motion and carried their gear in a standard fashion. As they practiced, they internalized the warning, "Use your hands. Use your feet. Use your head."[56]

Cargo Landing Net Given Its Initiation. Reprinted from *The Western Signal Corps Message* (Camp Kohler, CA, 7 October 1943) p. 1

Infiltration Course

Explosion on Infiltration Course. Reprinted from *The Western Signal Corps Message* (Camp Kohler, CA, 26 August 1943) p. 5.

In November 1943 the WSCRTC opened a new, action filled infiltration course, where "battle atmosphere with realistic scenes and sounds would bring combat conditions closer to trainees. The new infiltration course where battle atmosphere with realistic scenes and sounds would bring combat conditions closer to trainees. The new infiltration course near the rifle range"[57] included two .30 caliber machine guns showering live rounds rattling 36 inches over the heads of soldiers. The course was 350 feet long by 100 feet wide toward one end and fanned out to 150 feet at the other end. Beginning from a trench at the wide end, trainees ran upright for around 30 yards to a double aproned barbed wire fence. As they hit the ground to climb under the fence, the machine gun fire began. The following 60 yards was essentially secured in closeness to the ground. However, to keep the course from becoming routine, 12 pits gushed mud and water blasts at convenient intervals. Next soldiers confronted another barbed wire obstacle and made a crawling dive for the last trench, all the while dodging the water-cooled machine gun fire and explosions produced by a 23-foot control were at the narrow end near the finish line.

Lt. Col. Hover Goes under Barbed Wire on Infiltration Course. Reprinted from *The Western Signal Corps Message*, (Camp Kohler, CA, 26 August 1943) p. 5.

Swimming Pool

Davis Soldiers with Rifles in Pool. Reprinted from *The Western Signal Corps Message*, (25 May 1944, Camp Kohler CA) p. 4

Camp Kohler got its own swimming pool in April 1944. The pool was a good size at 120 feet long and 60 feet wide and a depth of 4 to 10 feet deep. Swimming was incorporated into the physical conditioning program. Stress was placed on emergency lifesaving methods, such as inflation of clothing or using laundry bags for temporary life preservers. Red Cross standards of teaching and testing were employed. The pool, located near the hospital and the main parade ground, was funded by profits from purchases at the Post Exchange.[58]

Feet First for Air. Inflated trousers keep GIs afloat. (Reprinted from *The Western Signal Corps Message,* (Camp Kohler, CA, 4 Nov. 1943) p. 5

ENTERTAINMENT FOR TROOPS

Off-duty soldiers took advantage of many different activities both on and off post. In addition to watching movies shown on the post, the soldiers participated in sports as well as music and drama. They also held dances and contests.

SPORTS PROGRAMS

Camp Kohler, by its sheer number of trainees and size, provided an opportunity for all types of athletic programs for soldiers. Kohler fielded sports teams in baseball, basketball, softball, touch football, boxing, golf, bowling, volleyball, and ping pong. Some of the sports teams were part of the Central California Servicemen's League. The camp appointed its very own athletic officer, Lt. Roy W. Long in October 1942. The Western Signal Corps School at Davis was also an active participant in sports programs for soldiers.

Camp Kohler Hosted a Wide Array of Sports Teams. Reprinted from *A Camera Trip Through Camp Kohler* (Camp Kohler, CA, August 1943).

Soldiers Play Baseball in Front of Camp Kohler Barracks. Signal Corps photo reprinted in *A Camera Trip Through Camp Kohler.* (Brooklyn NY, August 1943).

ORCHESTRA, BAND, AND GLEE CLUB

Besides sports for soldiers, Camp Kohler supported a music department. Its orchestra and band played on post as well as off post for public events. Many of the soldiers in the orchestra and band had played in professional bands prior to WWII. Camp Kohler had a glee club that sang on and off post as well.

The Camp Kohler Glee Club. Signal Corps photo reprinted in *A Camera Trip Through Camp Kohler (Brooklyn, NY, August 1943).*

CELEBRITIES PERFORM AT CAMP KOHLER

The headline read, "Hollywood is coming to Camp Kohler!" Capt. R.F. Tankersley, WSCRTC special service officer, announced that the performance was made possible through the efforts of the Hollywood Victory Committee. This was the very first show held on 17 April 1943 in the recreation hall at Kohler. "Heading the brilliant all-star cast [was] fiery Lucille Ball, who will exchange sharp remarks with jovial, Spanish-speaking Leo Carrillo; handsome, South American Desi Arnaz, [sic] and lovely Ann Ayres, bright starlet of Metro-Goldwyn-Mayer."[59] There were only 1300 tickets for the performance, so loudspeakers were placed outside of the building for those unable to obtain tickets. Tankersley went on to say that "it is hoped it will be the first of many such entertainments."[60]

These were not the only well-known personalities to come to Kohler. Several soldiers got their start in Hollywood before coming through the front gate. Playwright, novelist, and short story writer William Saroyan, whose play *The Time of Your Life*, won the Pulitzer Prize, received his basic training at Camp Kohler, and was further assigned to the Signal Corps photographic laboratory at Astoria, Long Island, New York. There, he wrote a script for *Screen Magazine*, a production that would be shown to the Army, Navy, and Marine Corps. Another Hollywood writer stationed at Camp Kohler for basic training was Louis Kaye, a script writer for comedian Bob Hope. He, too, was eventually assigned to Astoria, Long Island, New York, to work on movies for the Signal Corps. Furthermore, a Hollywood actor who appeared in the *Dead End Kids*, Don Latorre, was a sergeant in the special service branch at Camp Kohler and put on entertainment at the post. Also, *Wake Island* star, Jack Albertson, was a volunteer Signal Corps officer candidate at Camp Kohler. Furthermore, movie star Stanley Parlan completed Signal Corps training at Kohler. His movie *Ten Gentlemen from West Point* was filmed in 1942 and played at the camp movie theater during October 1943. In addition, though not an actor, Cpl. Fred Brooks, Jr. had been a scenery designer for a motion picture studio prior to his Army service. When speaking about Hollywood prop man, Pvt. Ralph D. Swartz, the camp newspaper, the *Message*, said, "And his words, mind you, are backed by 6 ½ years at Paramount and RKO where he helped build miniatures, action people, models, breakaway glass and furniture, etc."[61] Finally, Pvt. John Kearney, prior to his military service at Davis, acted in George M. Cohen's Broadway production *I'd Rather Be Right*. He had opted out of Hollywood to act in live theater.

BEAUTY CONTEST

In May 1943 it was announced that Camp Kohler was going to have a contest to name a Camp Kohler beauty queen. The contest would be held on 8 June at the post dance for enlisted men at the main recreation hall. Eight privates from the various training companies judged the 18 contestants and chose the winners: Miss Camp Kohler, Miss Faith Cathcart, 18, of Sacramento; 1st runner up, Miss Lea Peterson, 20, a McClellan Field secretary; and second runner up, Miss Vida Aldana, 17, member of the graduating class of Sacramento High School.[62]

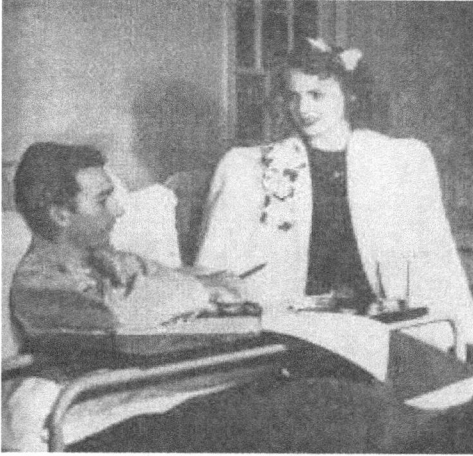

Miss Camp Kohler Speaks to a Soldier in the Station Hospital.
Reprinted from *The Western Signal Corps Message* (Camp Kohler, CA, (17 June 1943), p. 5.

OTHER SOLDIER SERVICES

TELEPHONE AND LIBRARY

The summer of 1943 brought even more services to Camp Kohler. In June 1943, the camp got its very own service men's telephone center through Pacific Telephone and Telegraph Company. Located in the rear half of the Bank of America building, the center had ten telephone booths with four lines dedicated to long distance and the other six lines for long distance and local calls. In addition, during the week of 28 June, the Camp Kohler library got its initial shipment of some 500 new fiction and nonfiction books. The post librarian, Ms. Mary Brice, arrived at Camp Kohler after attending a two-week training course at Fort Douglas, Utah. Furthermore, on 26 August 1943, a new beer garden opened adjacent to the main post exchange.

Soldiers Could Relax in the Library with a Good Book. Signal Corps Photo reprinted in *A Camera Trip Through Camp Kohler.* (Brooklyn, NY, August 1943).

LOCAL TRANSPORTATION

The soldiers sometimes found entertainment in town, often at the USO, so Camp Kohler came up with its own system of convoying soldiers to and from Sacramento for off duty relaxation. Camp officials felt bus service was inadequate, so they created a plan which permitted soldiers to reach Sacramento without violating camp regulations against hitchhiking. According to the *Sacramento Bee*, "A ten truck convoy, accommodating approximately 150 soldiers, [left the camp] nightly at 6:30 p.m. for Sacramento and [started] the return trip from the

USO at Ninth and I Streets at 10:30 p.m."[63] The Gibson Bus Line also helped many soldiers and airman get to and from Sacramento from their bases during the war years. In February 1943, Gibson added 16 additional departures from the post as compared to 10 in the past and 15 additional departures from Sacramento as compared to 13 in the past.

SERVICEMEN, THE COMMUNITY, AND THE COUNTRY

Servicemen Wait in Line to Board a Bus for Sacramento. Signal Corps Photo reprinted in *A Camera Trip Through Camp Kohler.* (Brooklyn, NY, August 1943).

Servicemen participated in activities that benefitted both the community and the country. Because the lack of employees during war years affected local agriculture, soldiers responded on at least two occasions. First on 25 September 1942, their day off, 500 Camp Kohler soldiers provided community service by helping to pick tomatoes on local farms. The farm owners provided transportation for soldiers going to the fields.[64] Again, as a service to the public, in August 1943, the U.S. Employment Service and officers at the Davis WSCS made an agreement to allow soldier students to work in the Matmor cannery (later Del Monte) in Woodland, California, to help relieve certain labor shortages due to the war. These volunteer soldiers would work the evening shift during the peak season and would be paid the established wage.[65]

In addition, soldiers strongly supported the American Red Cross with their generous contributions and participated actively in the War Bond program, even enlisting the help of civilians in raising funds to support the war effort. Also, Army service force personnel used their equipment to further the war effort by assisting in the collection of scrap metal during Camp Kohler's scrap metal drives.

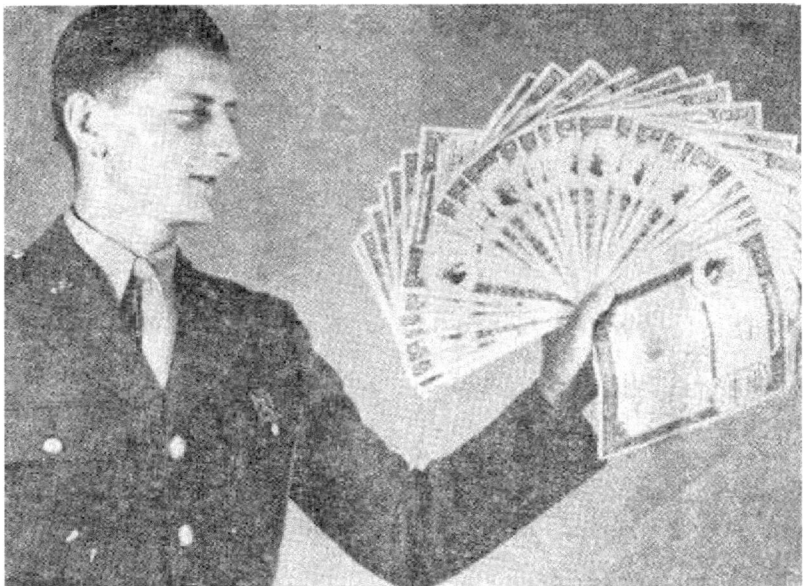

A Soldier Displays His War Bonds in His Hands Like a Hand of Poker. Reprinted from *The Western Signal Corps Message*, (Camp Kohler, CA, 30 September 1943), p. 1.

Furthermore, on 13 October 1943, Camp Kohler opened its doors for a tour of the camp by local business leaders, *Sacramento* newspaper personnel, wire service personnel, and radio men. Finally, Camp Kohler had its own radio program over Sacramento KFBK radio with tunes and public information.

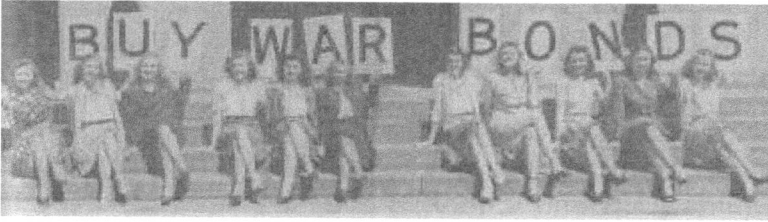

Students of Sigma Iota Chi Sorority, of Sacramento City College, Lined Up for This Patriotic Motif in conjunction with Camp Kohler's Fifth War Bond Campaign. *The Western Signal Corps Message,* (Camp Kohler, CA, 8 June 1944) p.1.

SPECIALIZED TRAINING AT THE WESTERN SIGNAL CORPS SCHOOL (WSCS), DAVIS

Until January 1943, trainees graduating from basic training at Camp Kohler had to go to either Fort Monmouth or Camp Crowder for specialized training because there was nothing available at Camp Kohler. To solve the problem of a lack of specialized training at Camp Kohler, General Sherrill, commander of the WSCRTC at Kohler started to look at potential locations for an additional Signal Corps school. In October 1942, Sherrill directed Capt. (later Maj.) Francis G. Sanning, chief of the signal communications branch stationed at Kohler, to make a survey of existing facilities within 200 miles of Camp Kohler. The Signal Corps needed a campus type facility with billeting, classrooms, dining facilities, physical fitness facilities, and training areas. The University of California, College of Agriculture at Davis, fourteen miles west of Sacramento, met the selection criteria. General Sherrill forwarded his recommendation to the chief signal officer for approval on 22 November 1942. The commanding general, services of supply (SOS) authorized the establishment of a new Western Signal Corps School in Davis.[66]

Camp Kohler subsequently became the headquarters for the WSCRTC, comprising both the WSCRTC at Camp Kohler and the WSCS at Davis. During the fall of 1942, the U.S. Army negotiated with university president Robert Sproul for the use of the Davis campus as a military training school. The Army proposed to obtain the necessary classroom and housing facilities by lease, and the Signal Corps would supply the necessary instructional equipment. The University of California would retain sufficient space and facilities to continue research on experimental farms currently being operated. College students at the agricultural school were to complete their present semester's studies during January 1943, prior to the commencement of full operations by the WSCS. By 1 January 1943 the entire Davis campus was officially converted into a training facility for the WSCS.

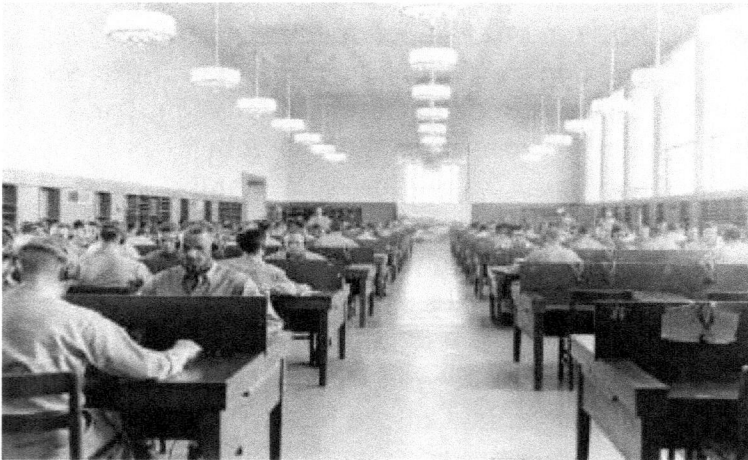

WSCS Soldiers Training in Morse Code in the Former Shields Library at the UC College of Agriculture, Davis. (Photo courtesy of the National Archives).

The WSCS, administered as a subunit of Camp Kohler, took over the dormitories, the gymnasium and swimming pool, and most of the academic buildings. The library became the radio school. The first commandant of the

WSCS was LtC. Edward A. Allen, who had previously served as the chief of staff, Central Signal Corps Training Center at Camp Crowder. Official activation of the WSCS at Davis took place on 11 January 1943 per General Order #1, Headquarters, Western Signal Corps School, Davis, CA.[67] The capacity of the WSCS was established at 1,000 students and the specialist training courses offered at Davis would be radio and telegraph operation and radio repair. The Army requested an allotment of 30 officers to provide for staff and faculty and 244 non-commissioned officers and enlisted personnel for administrative support. The first group of 100 students began training the week February 1943 in low- and high-speed radio operator courses.[68]

Repeater Carrier Terminal Training Which Is Part of the WSCS Specialist Training Program. Reprinted from *Western Signal Corps Message* (Camp Kohler CA, 9 December 1943) p. 5.

A Soldier Training on the Telephone Central Office Installation Curriculum at Davis. Reprinted from *The Western Signal School Message,* (Camp Kohler, CA, 9 December 1943) p. 5

All students in training were housed in campus dormitories. "Enlisted instructor cadre men for the most part [were] housed in college fraternity houses in Davis outside the actual boundary of the campus."[69] One fraternity house served as bachelor officers' quarters and a downtown hotel was used when necessary. A movie theater was set up in a former lecture hall at Davis. Also, two post exchanges were set up, one in a former student co-op store and the other in a *rathskeller* in the basement of one of the dormitories. As a regular part of the schedule at Davis, a 75mm. French field piece (cannon), located in the northeast corner of the campus quadrangle pointing in a northerly direction, was added to the daily regulation reveille and retreat ceremonies.[70]

New trainees arriving at Davis received a student guide that told them what to expect while in training. The guide told them about Saturday inspections and other campus services, such as $0.45 haircuts at the post barber shop and laundry service for $1.50 per month. Movies could be viewed for $0.15 on campus and round-trip tickets from Davis to San Francisco cost $1.95.[71]

Western Signal Corps School Students Line Up on the UC Davis Quad. Yolo County Archives/Larkey collection. Courtesy, YOLO COUNTY ARCHIVES. Date assessed August 25, 2017.

Seven buildings at the College of Agriculture, University of California, Davis, were renamed by the WSCS. The buildings were renamed in honor of former chief of signal officers of the United States Army as follows: Administration Building: Meyer Hall for BG. Albert J. Meyer (1860-1863, 1866-1880); Agricultural Engineering: Hazen Hall for BG. William B. Hazen (1880-1887); Dairy Industry Building: Greely Hall for MG. Adolphus W. Greely

(1887-1906), also an Artic explorer; Animal Science Building: Allen Hall for BG. James Allen (1906-1913); Old Gymnasium: Scriven Hall for BG. George Scriven (1913-1917); Chemistry Building: Squier Hall for MG. George O. Squier (1917-1923); and Horticulture Building: Saltzman Hall for MG. Charles M. Saltzman (1924-1928).[72]

Nerve Center of Western Signal Corps School, Davis. Reprinted from *The Western Signal Corps Message*, (Camp Kohler, CA, 25 February 1943), p. 1.

REPLACEMENT TRAINING CENTERS CONVERTED TO UNIT TRAINING CENTERS

By 1944, the replacement training centers had outlasted their missions, so they would convert to unit training centers. Signal Corps replacement training became concentrated at Camp Crowder, which provided all loss replacements and other individual specialists as were needed. The Eastern Signal Corps Replacement Training Center (ESCRTC) at Fort Monmouth was discontinued and the Eastern Signal Corps Unit Training Center (ESCUTC) was organized on 10 August 1943 while the WSCRTC at Camp Kohler was discontinued on 31 December 1943 and the Western Signal Corps Unit Training Center (WSCUTC) was organized on 1 January 1944.[73]

When the unit type training was instituted at the WSCRTC on 14 December 1943, the basic branch, which had been instructing trainees in basic military subjects, was disbanded. Colonel Storms, commander of the new Kohler unit training center announced, "...reorganization of the camp from a replacement training center to a unit training center."[74] Now each training company would handle the entire training program for its members. The new mission was to take in "...raw recruits and turn out fully trained teams of specialists."[75] That implied preparing new arrivals for basic training, teaching them basic soldier skills, and turning them into new specialists that would then attend special schools. Afterwards, each of these highly trained soldiers would become part of a team, with soldiers of many specialties working together. To put it plainly, the transformation of RTC's into UTC's did not include an overnight change in capacity, but rather only a readjustment of duties and functions.

The transformation from group instruction to unit type training was made gradually so that the training program would not be delayed in any way. The shift was complete by 6 January 1944. Camp Kohler's signal communications branch would provide initial instruction for pole linemen, low speed radio operators, and common battery telephone switchboard operators. Some of the first trainees were members of the Army Air Forces, who were being trained by the Signal Corps. In addition, the 840th Signal Training Battalion, with its 20 training companies, a headquarters company, and four provisional battalion headquarters teams, was transferred to Camp Kohler from Camp Crowder less personnel and equipment (in other words, in name only.) (See APPENDIX B for a list of other units at Camp Kohler.)

The Signal Corps unit training centers were established for the activation and training of Signal Corps tactical organizations. Men with no service training and soldiers trained by Signal Corps schools were formed into Signal Corps units. New soldiers received six weeks of basic training. Then from the seventh through the fourteenth week, soldiers received training which was oriented towards technical training. A specialty was assigned to all trainees. Trainees were taught the proper nomenclature, capabilities, and limitations of their assigned equipment. They learned about component parts along with operation precautions. At the completion of the training period, soldiers were qualified as apprentices in their assigned duty assignments. They had to be able to perform their assigned skill at a higher level to undertake training as a member of a team. Therefore, field training exercises were conducted during the fifteenth and seventeenth weeks. Trainees continued to participate in field exercises, honing their skills as a member of a team. When the unit completed its training, it would be sent to the theater where the unit mission was required.

Signal Corps training centers tried to offer all types of training to students. One type of training not readily available was operating communications equipment at the installation level. Eventually the major signal training centers set up an entire simulated theater level communications system for trainee's practicum. Cellular teams operated a network system and various signal facilities and signal centers. "By mid-1944, the Kohler Theater Headquarters Signal Center included a message center, teletypewriter, radio receiving and transmitting positions for remote operations, and a code room well equipped with cryptographic devices."[76] Trainees from this center were responsible for keeping communications with the 20th Army Group (Phantom) at Camp Kohler headquarters which was placed a half a mile away with the same equipment, and responsible for communications with the Camp Crowder phantom theater headquarters.

The WSCS at Davis acted as a base section headquarters. All the sections were to respond to phony message traffic prepared by trainees.

Training sections were all equipped with telephone communications through the Camp Kohler telephone

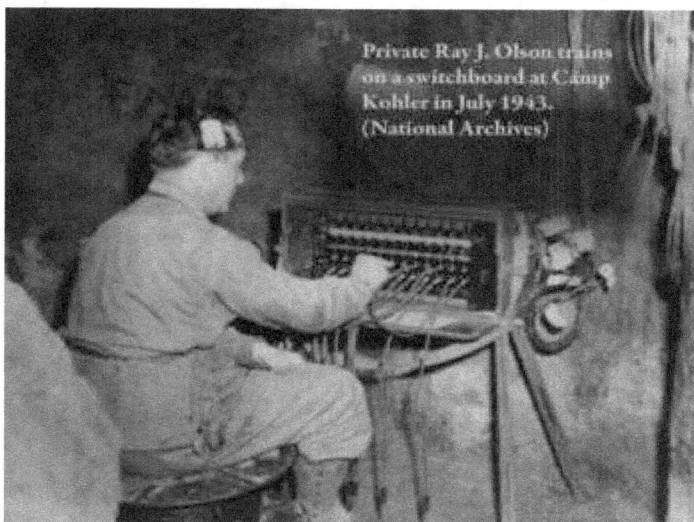

Private Ray J. Olson trains on a switchboard at Camp Kohler in July 1943. (National Archives)

training system (known as the Cobra Exchange) which was handled through leased commercial lines. When the post telephone system could not handle the volume of trainee traffic, Camp Kohler used the Cobra Exchange which had been built earlier to train switchboard operators and maintenance personnel. Kohler later established the Rambler Exchange to allow for a new telephone training center. To provide for conditions similar to what soldiers might have to live and work in overseas, Kohler built a rhombic receiving area (antenna area), telephone pole construction area, telephone switchboard and teletypewriter, and network of five simulated headquarters.[77]

Students Climbing and Training on Telephone Poles at Camp Kohler. (U.S. Army Signal Corps photo reprinted in *Radio News, Special Signal Corps Issue,* Vol. 28, No 5, Nov. 1942, p. 82.

THE HANDWRITING ON THE WALL

On 21 February 1944 an article appeared in the *Sacramento Bee* regarding men being transferred to combat units. It said, "Col. Harry E. Storms, commanding officer of the Western Signal Corps Training Center at Camp Kohler, announced today all able bodied enlisted men under 38 who have been handling office work and other camp duties will be transferred to combat field units by June 30th."[78] Civilian personnel, Women's Army Corps personnel who were not physically qualified for overseas duty, and replacements having just returned from overseas duty would take over these positions. Col. Storms' action was in line with the War Department policy of rotating men from combat areas to fill jobs on domestic installations.

Loading Army Jeeps on Railroad Flat Car for Shipment
reprinted in *The Western Signal Corps Message,* (Camp Kohler, CA, 7 Sept 1944) p.1.

Within six months, even with classes still in session at Camp Kohler and Davis, the Army declared Camp Kohler surplus on August 10th with an effective date of 31 October 1944. At the same time, the Ninth Service Command ordered a nine-hour work day for both military and civilian employees working at Kohler and its allied post at the College of Agriculture in Davis, Yolo County, because of a backlog of work in the Army service forces and because the two installations would soon be closing.[79] Civilians were compensated for the extra hours worked. On 31 October 1944 the WSCUTC at Camp Kohler and the WSCS at Davis were discontinued. At this point, actions were taken to curtail training; transfer staff, faculty and students; and ship equipment to Camp Crowder or Fort Monmouth.

The station hospital closed in October 1944 as well. The last edition of the Camp Kohler Message reported on 14 October that the hospital had treated a record 11,290 patients in its existence from 1942-1944. There had been only 18 deaths of which 11 had been accidental.[80] One of those accidents had occurred on 26 November 1943 when a Davis signal trainee was electrocuted as his radio antenna touched an overhead high-tension wire during a field training exercise.

THE MESSAGE FINISHES ITS RUN

The Western Signal Corps Message, the official organ of the WSCUTC at Camp Kohler and the WSCS at Davis began as a single mimeographed sheet. Published each Thursday, it had a reader population ranging from

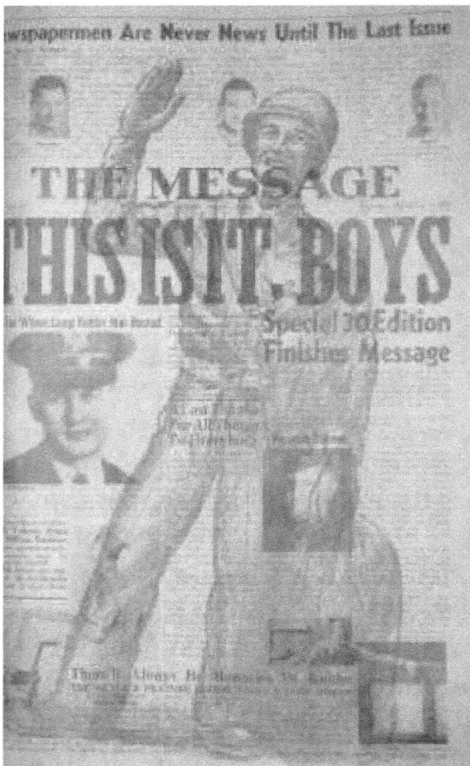

Front Cover of the Last *Western Signal Corps Message* (Camp Kohler, CA,14 September 1944), p. 1.

6,500 to 10,000 since it came into being in October 1942. The 170th and final edition of The *Western Signal Corps Message* was printed on 15 September 1944 by the *Auburn Journal*, Auburn, CA. The illustrated souvenir edition of the Signal Corps "city" depicted the histories and functions of the various camp units and its former commanders along with its front page carrying a double printed colored sketch of GI Joe saying, "So long!"[81]

COMMANDERS AND SUCCESSORS

Over the course of a few years, Camp Kohler had several commanders. On 11 March 1943 Brigadier General Sherrill completed his tenure at Kohler to become the next commanding general of the Eastern Signal Corps Training Center (ESCTC) at Fort Monmouth. He relinquished command to the temporary custody of Col. R.W. McNamee, executive officer, until Col. Harry E.

BG Steven H. Sherrill
(*The Message)*

Col. Harry E. Storms
(*The Message)*

Storms assumed command on 5 April 1943. Storms had previously been assigned as signal officer of the Caribbean Defense Command in 1942. His most recent assignments had been at Camp Crowder, at Fort Monmouth, and in the office of chief signal officer in Washington, DC.[82]

When Colonel Storms departed 10 June 1944 for a new assignment as commandant of schools at Fort Monmouth, Col. James W. Green, Jr. replaced him at Camp Kohler.[83]

Col. James W. Green, Jr. (*The Message*)

Green had started the first radar school in the United States and his last duty assignment prior to Kohler was as commander for three and one-half years at the southern Signal Corps training school at Camp Murphy, Florida.[84]

Col. John L. Autrey, (*The Message*)

By early August 1944, Colonel Green had left his post at Kohler for an overseas assignment, to be replaced temporarily by Col. John L. Autrey on 16 August 1944. Autrey had previously returned from 20 months in Australia and New Guinea and his last duty assignment had been at Camp Crowder.[85]

Col. Hugh Mitchell, (*The Message)*

On 7 September 1944 Col. Hugh Mitchell replaced Autrey who returned to Camp Crowder. Mitchell had only recently returned from the Southwest Pacific where he had been a Signal Corps officer for the services of supply. When the WSCUTC closed, Colonel Mitchell was reassigned as commandant of schools at the Eastern Signal Corps School at Fort Monmouth.[86]

Col. Edward A. Allen, (*The Message*)

The original commandant at the WSCS at Davis, Col. Edward A. Allen, who had been on board since January 1943, departed Davis in March 1944, for a new assignment at Camp Campbell, Kentucky. Allen, who had been promoted to colonel in October 1943, was replaced by LtC. James H. Ferrick, acting commandant until Davis closed on 31 October 1944. Ferrick had served as the executive officer of the WSCTC since September 1942.[87] (See APPENDIX C for a list of key military and civilian personnel.)

ARMY AIR FORCES (AAF) MOVES IN

The AAF had become aware early on that Kohler would be available for conversion to an overseas replacement depot which would receive and process men for shipment to overseas air forces. During the week of 23 October 1944, Washington made a pronouncement that the AAF would assume control over Camp Kohler. The War Department's declaration showed plans had, indeed, been made to utilize Kohler for the final push of AAF personnel before they were sent into the Asiatic-Pacific Theater. Nevertheless, Signal Corps officials at the post said they had not been formally notified with respect to this transfer of function; they did not know how long the Signal Corps would stay on at the camp. On 24 October 1944 Representative Leroy Johnson, third congressional district, sent a telegram to the *Sacramento Bee* saying, "Camp Kohler removed from surplus property list and placed under jurisdiction of Army Air Forces and will become active."[88] The War Department issued orders dating back to 10 August 1944 declaring Kohler surplus with an effective date of 31 October 1944. On 1

November 1944 when queried by the media on the future status of Kohler, officials at the camp stated that "...they are 'standing by' awaiting information from Washington on the question of turning the military field over to the AAF for use as a staging area."[89]

The AAF took over the Camp Kohler installation under the AAF's personnel distribution command in mid-December 1944. On that date Camp Kohler was further assigned to the AAF replacement depot, Kearns, Utah, for operation and administration. The only wrinkle here was that it was to be temporarily placed in an inactive status pending its being made an active installation again. Effective 16 December 1944 Maj. Clarence R. Case, AAF, arrived and took temporary command of Camp Kohler pending the arrival of Maj. Gilson A. McNeill from Kearns, Utah. McNeill took official command of Kohler on 2 January 1945, and Case became the public relations officer. The camp was under the jurisdiction of Colonel Weldon W. Doe, commanding officer of the overseas replacement depot at Kearns, Utah.

While in inactive status, Kohler was the site of the California State Guard spring encampment of the California High School Cadet Corps from 24 March through 31 March 1945. Approximately 600 cadets from 101 high schools throughout the state participated during their Easter vacation period. Cadets underwent a normal military training schedule under the supervision of the California State Guard. The AAF, which had jurisdiction over Kohler, granted authority for the encampment.[90]

On 18 May 1945 General Order No. 18, HQ, AAF, Personnel Distribution Command, at Louisville, Kentucky, finally placed Camp Kohler in active status. It became the fourth AAF overseas replacement depot in the country, with others in Kearns, Utah; Greensboro, North Carolina; and Santa Ana, California. When Major McNeill returned to

Kearns, Utah, AAF Maj. Nels O. Olsen was put in charge of Camp Kohler.[91]

GERMAN PRISONER OF WAR ESCAPES

On 13 July 1945 Georg Gerst, 25, a German prisoner of war, temporarily assigned to the Camp Kohler work detail from the Stockton, California, prisoner of war camp, escaped. On 17 July 1945 Gerst was spotted by four boys aged 7 to 10, who pretended to be playing a short distance away. They quickly went to the police station to report their noticing of Gerst to Captain Joseph Zanolio, who reported this information to Camp Kohler and the FBI. The AAF sent a detail of 35 soldiers to find him. Gerst was found a quarter of a mile from where he was seen by the boys. He was shaving in the bottom of Dry Creek near Roseville and did not resist being taken into custody.[92]

ARMY TAKES CAMP KOHLER BACK

It was a mere six months in an active status as an AAF overseas replacement depot when the Army came knocking. Effective 15 November 1945 Camp Kohler was transferred from the jurisdiction of the AAF to the commanding general, Army service forces, reclassified from a Class III to a Class IV installation under the command of the chief of transportation to operate as a sub-post of the San Francisco (SF) port of embarkation effective 22 January 1946.[93] With the Christmas holidays rapidly approaching in December 1945, and with the war over in Europe and the Pacific, a lot of soldiers and airman were being discharged and wanted to get home for the holidays.

In early January 1946, Col. Harry J. Farner took command of the Camp Kohler Port of Embarkation which was operating as a branch of Camp Stoneman under the overall command of the SF Port of Embarkation at Fort

Mason. Camp Stoneman would remain an active installation until 1954. (See Appendix C: Key Military and Civilian Leadership.)

The SF port of embarkation declared Camp Kohler (3,453 acres[94]) surplus on 1 March 1946, and by 19 March 1946 the *Sacramento Bee* announced, "the Army Corps of Engineers, Sacramento district [would assume] responsibility for disposition under the army's surplus property regulations" with some exceptions.[95] More specifically, the quartermaster laundry consisting of 72,173 square feet of building space was placed under the jurisdiction of the AAF, McClellan Field. The Walerga engineer sub-depot and an adjoining site were placed under the jurisdiction of the Army ground forces for post war reserve activities. Nevertheless, a contingent of some 10 officers and some 50 enlisted men of the SF port of embarkation remained at Kohler as a maintenance force. Other personnel from the SF port of embarkation which had operated Kohler for six months as a branch of Camp Stoneman returned to Stoneman. On 4 May 1946 the commanding general, SF port of embarkation finally transferred for disposition the remaining portions of Camp Kohler to the district engineer, Sacramento, California. (See APPENDIX D: War Department Inventory of Owned, Sponsored, and Leased Facilities.)

JAPANESE AMERICANS RETURN TO KOHLER

After the war, Japanese American evacuees returning to the Sacramento region had been scheduled to arrive on 30 October 1945, but they were delayed because of the inability to find housing. They finally arrived on 9 November. Early arrivals had already been living in overcrowded hostels, but those who arrived later could not find accommodations. With the help of the US Army liaison officer, the federal public housing administration, and the WRA, families could use the barracks at Camp

Kohler until they could find other living quarters. Block 56 was remodeled and renovated for the return of Japanese Americans, and families began moving into apartments in block 56 at Allen Street and Monmouth Avenue at the camp. The set capacity of 234 persons was reached by the end of November 1945. Many people in the community protested the use of Camp Kohler for Japanese housing. On 3 November the Sacramento Chamber of Commerce called it "almost criminal," insisting that the facilities be held for returning veterans and their families.[96] In addition, on 10 November the California Veterans of Foreign Wars (VFW) "vigorously protest use of Camp Kohler for use of returning Japanese from relocation centers until all returning veterans are provided with proper housing facilities."[97] Nevertheless, the Japanese were allowed to remain temporarily.

1945 TO 1972

WALERGA SUB-DEPOT ESTABLISHED

Not all of Camp Kohler was held by the Army or AAF. On 1 May 1945 the establishment of the Walerga engineer depot, which would serve as a sub-depot of the Lathrop engineer depot, Lathrop, California was announced. It was organized as a Class IV installation under the jurisdiction of the chief of engineers.[98] "The Walerga engineer depot consisted of a lumberyard with a railroad spur line from the main Southern Pacific Line," as shown on the 1945 Layout Plan. "There was storage on both sides of the spur and two additional sidings."[99] In spring 1945, it was announced by the Sacramento district office Corps of Engineers that waste lumber was available for sale at their Walerga lumberyard at Camp Kohler. The wood, suitable for fireplaces, was being sold at $2.00 for a 1½ to 2-ton truck load. Then on 1 March 1946 Walerga was re-designated as the Walerga engineer sub-depot of the retitled Lathrop Army service forces depot and placed under the technical jurisdiction of the engineer supply officer at Lathrop. Just twelve days later the title for Walerga was amended to read Walerga sub-depot and remained under the jurisdiction of the chief of engineers. Effective 25 September 1946 Walerga sub-depot was reclassified a Class II sub-installation assigned to the Stockton general depot under the jurisdiction of the quartermaster general. The quartermaster general finally made plans to discontinue the Walerga sub-depot as of 30 June 1948.[100]

The Walerga sub-depot gained a bit of notoriety in 1947. Victor Lamken, a materials dealer, had been charged with theft of government property in May 1946 for the removal of 38,800 pounds of sandbags from the Army depot at Stockton, San Joaquin County. He had also been charged with bribery on 14 November 1946 when he offered Captain Virgil S. Wade, officer in charge of the Army engineers' Walerga depot, $1000 to declare certain materials surplus. He was arrested immediately after he had made a $50 down payment on the bribe. Lamken was indicted in January 1947 on both counts. A jury found Lamken guilty on both charges and federal judge Dal M. Lemmon sentenced him on 14 April 1947 to 18 months in jail on the bribery charge and fined him $1,500 on the second charge of stealing government property. The bribery charge also carried a mandatory fine of $50.[101] [102]

OTHER EVENTS IN THE LIFE OF CAMP KOHLER

A large fire engulfed portions of Camp Kohler on 20 June 1947. The fire destroyed an estimated 50 buildings at Kohler and up to 20 dwellings near the post. Ten suburban fire departments, state forestry firefighters, and two military airfield fire departments with over 300 men and equipment along with the only few soldiers remaining at Kohler at the time brought the blaze under control. As reported in the *Sacramento Bee*, "More than 50 persons were treated for burns and injuries."[103] One of the Arcade volunteer firefighters, Charles Gay, died of third degree burns. David Westerman, chief of the Hagginwood fire department, said that the fire apparently started in grass near Camp Kohler."[104] Another theory attributes the fire to a Southern Pacific train. After the fire spread through the camp, the fire went south and east through the grass. According to the *Sacramento Bee,* "The tar paper and wooden barracks structures at Camp Kohler parched bone dry in the summer sun, burned like tinder and were said by fireman to be responsible for the eight-mile width of the fire front attained."[105] Winds reaching 47 miles per hour fanned the flames.

In October 1947, because "the sale of the buildings was under legislation authority for the state to buy war surplus buildings for resale to veterans,"[106] the California State Finance Department, Allocation Division, began to sell off the Camp Kohler buildings. Sales began on 8 October and continued through 13 October. The state department of finance announced on 14 October that all but seven of 231 Camp Kohler buildings had been sold to veterans. The buildings sold included barracks, recreation rooms, mess halls, and the post hospital. Purchasers had 30 days in which to dismantle the buildings and move them from the camp. In December 1948, the allocation division, state of California sold an additional 37 buildings of 39 available. The *Sacramento Bee* indicated the demand for these buildings when it reported that some "housing hungry veterans" had stood in line for two days to make sure they could take advantage of the first come, first served sale.[107] Later, in 1952 and 1955, the Sacramento district Corps of Engineers sold more buildings to the public. Shortages of building materials had made these structures valuable.

In September 1948, some structures still existed when the California Air National Guard 146th Aircraft

Control and Warning Squadron was activated with its headquarters at Camp Kohler, and in November, the California Army National Guard also moved in. The National Guard said "The state recently acquired 32 acres of the tract as well as 10 buildings and eight warehouses. The buildings will serve as classrooms, administrative headquarters, and a service center and storage space."[108] The units that joined the 146th Squadron at Camp Kohler were the 636th Field Artillery, 184th Infantry, and the 126th Medical Detachment.

In January 1949, St. Rose's Catholic Church in Roseville "purchased the Camp Kohler chapel and planned to move it to Citrus Heights".[109] Two months later, the church found a suitable three-acre tract on Auburn Boulevard near Sunrise Avenue. The members tore down the chapel, hauled it to the new location, and reassembled it.[110]

On 18 January 1951 the AAF was considering reactivating Camp Kohler to active status as a basic training center. It would be used for a basic indoctrination course of six weeks and would have 30,000 military and civilian personnel. MG. William McKee, assistant vice chief of staff, Air Force, contacted United States Senator William Knowland of California about the use of the camp. Senator Knowland contacted Sacramento mayor Bert E. Geisreiter about whether Sacramento "...can absorb such a force with adequate housing and other necessary facilities."[111] The mayor and the city council took a favorable position supporting reactivating Camp Kohler, and the Sacramento Chamber of Commerce president, Robert A. Breuner, said "Chamber officials herald the Camp Kohler reactivation program as a great step forward in the expansion of the Sacramento metropolitan area."[112] Additionally, on 26 January 1951 the Senate armed services committee recommended an appropriation of $64,261,999 to reactivate and build up Camp Kohler as an Air Force training base. Even Congressman Leroy Johnson of the third Sacramento district, notified the Chamber of Commerce "that $52,000,000 of the proposed appropriation would be used for airmen's housing."[113]

The Department of Defense (DoD) finally announced its decision on reactivating Camp Kohler on 25 April 1951. Unfortunately, it was not good news for Sacramento and the region. DoD chose not to reactivate Kohler; instead, it transferred to the Air Force two portions of Camp Shoemaker to be used for basic indoctrination training. Approximately 3,000 acres of land were involved in the transfer. Shoemaker had been a major WWII, Pacific Coast, U.S. Naval training and distribution center adjoining Camp Parks in Pleasanton. The installation would become Parks Air Force base.[114] The facts that Kohler had sold off many of its buildings, the fire had destroyed numbers of base structures in 1947, and it was going to cost $52,000,000 to build enlisted living quarters weighed heavily against Kohler's being reactivated as a training base.

In December 1958, a San Francisco Bay Area developer, David D. Bohannon, announced that he had purchased 1,340 acres of land in the North Highlands area of Sacramento County for residential, commercial, and industrial development. The $100 million-dollar development would include homes, apartments, shopping centers, schools, parks, and playgrounds. The land was purchased from Dean Dillman and his sister, Corrine Dillman Kirchhofer, both of San Francisco, who had been the primary lessors of the land comprising Camp Kohler. Approximately one-third of the Camp Kohler property was included in the purchase. Construction was to begin immediately on the first unit of some 300 homes.[115]

In 1959, the federal government decided to release its responsibility for the Camp Kohler sewage treatment plant. The *Sacramento Bee* reported, "Built in WW II at a cost of $128,770, local sub dividers have spent almost $500,000 expanding it in recent years."[116] Because the treatment plant had already been processing wastewater for subdivisions in North Highlands, Larchmont Villages, and Foothill Farms, the government decided to turn the treatment plant over to Sacramento County. The county had been leasing it for free for thirteen years in exchange for processing the sewage from the Kohler laundry and McClellan Air Force base. When the county agreed to continue to process the wastewater for the Air Force base for free, Congressman John E. Moss (D) third congressional district, Sacramento, introduced legislation to make the agreement legal, and President Dwight D. Eisenhower signed the bill into law. The facility was demolished in 1972.[117]

THE CAMP KOHLER AREA TODAY

What's left of the Sacramento assembly center and Camp Kohler? Not much of anything these days. The former assembly center area is now bisected by Interstate 80 and covered with housing subdivisions (including the subdivisions built by Bohannon) in what is now the Foothill Farms-North Highlands area of Sacramento.[118] There are a small group of cherry trees, a Ramada, and a plaque commemorating California Historical Landmark #934, Temporary Detention Camps for Japanese Americans – Sacramento Assembly Center, in Walerga Park at the northwest corner of Palm Avenue and College Oak Drive. Originally dedicated on 28 February 1987 the Walerga assembly center memorial was re-dedicated before a crowd of 200 people on 25 August 2015 after improvements and repairs were completed. Florin Japanese American Citizens League (JACL) worked on the re-dedication program with representatives from the

Sacramento JACL and the Sunrise recreation and park district.

California State Landmark #934 at Walerga Park Monument in Front of Ramada and Cherry Trees. Located at College Oak Drive and Palm Avenue, Sacramento, CA. Courtesy of Beverly Johnson.

In addition, there is a sign on Roseville Road that says, "Camp Kohler, 5922 Roseville Rd, Gate 201." It is next to a fenced area that has a building and a tower with a rotating antenna which were formerly part of Camp Kohler and later McClellan AFB. These have been transferred to the Federal Aviation Administration. There is also a large concrete foundation on this property that belonged to the former base laundry, which was burned to the ground in 1981 as a fire training exercise.

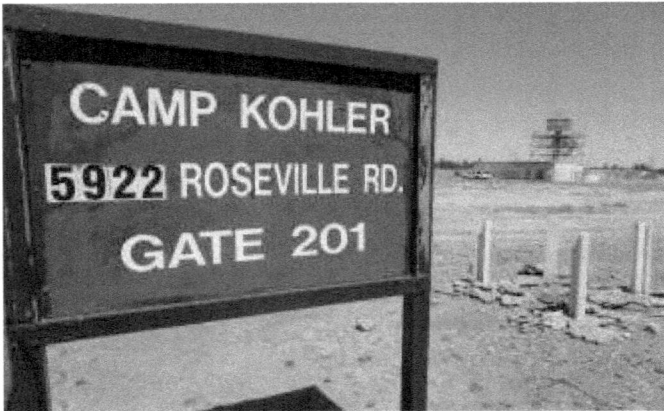

Camp Kohler Address Sign at the FAA Radar Facility at 5922 Roseville Road, Sacramento, CA. Photograph courtesy of Beverly Johnson.

Other parts of the post have been utilized as well. "The former site of the Camp Kohler station hospital is currently occupied by Foothills High School, which is part of the Grant Joint Union School District, and by residential housing between Merton Way and McCloud Drive."[119] The swimming pool became part of the high school. The site of the old parade ground is now Foothills Baptist Church, Robert Frost Park, and the Foothills High School football stadium, which sits directly on top of the "oiled and graveled area." This area was completely excavated during the construction of the stadium. The water tower, which would have been just west of the parking lot for Foothill Farms Junior High School, had been in disuse over the years, and the tank had become a haven for graffiti artists. According to the *Sacramento Bee*, "Its last practical use was to be set on fire for firefighters' practice," [120] and later demolished.

Former Site of Camp Kohler/McClellan AFB Laundry on Roseville Road, Sacramento, CA. Photograph courtesy of Beverly Johnson.

CONCLUSION

Camp Kohler had a short but interesting life span of just a few years. It started from scratch to become a polished military installation, answering the call each time its mission changed. The once meager facilities of Camp Kohler blossomed into a fully developed training center through which thousands of soldiers passed, prompting the expansion to the Western Signal Corps School in Davis, CA. Moreover, individual training eventually became unit training to serve the needs of the Signal Corps better, and experienced commanders added to a sound training environment. Furthermore, musical and stage productions performed by soldiers were followed by entertainment from Hollywood. Even transportation into town improved. Finally, when the Signal Corps no longer needed the camp, other branches of the Armed Forces took advantage of what the Army had built. Initially the

Walerga assembly center, Camp Kohler opened its doors for a second time to provide temporary housing for many Sacramento Japanese Americans who had no home to return to after their internment. Camp Kohler was a "can do" military installation of many uses. It truly "answered the call in time of war" to "get the message through" all over the world.

APPENDIX A: Camp Kohler Real Property Leases as of 15 April 1946[121]

Camp Kohler consisted of a total of 3,609.4012 acres of which the government leased 3,008.4 acres and controlled by permanent easements 1.0012 acres.

Lease No.

W2972-eng-1319

Lessor: H.B. Drescher and L. and B. Kleinsorge

W868-eng-1613

Lessor: C.D. Kirchofer and B. Dillman

W04-193-eng-2287

Lessor: Mattie B. Harris

W868-eng-1534

Lessor: Mattie B. Harris

W04-193-eng-2288:

Lessor: P. H. and Lila Guttman

W2972-eng-897

Lessor: Carl J. Peterson

W3460-eng-3803

Lessor: State of California

W3460-eng-3780

Lessor: Fred L. Dorman

Cond. Case No. 4556

Lessor: I.S. Haines

W04-193-eng-2738

Lessor: Frank and Angela Smith

W04-193-eng-1984

Lessor: Wm. H. and H.F. Bonham

W04-193-eng-1831

Lessor: George T. Dean

W04-193-eng-4160

Lessor: Frank and Anna Figearo

W04-193-eng-2583

Lessor: C. D. Kirchofer and D. Dillman

W3460-eng-3759

Lessor: M.L. and N.C. Roussin

W04-193-eng-1832

Lessor: L.B. Larkin and A.B. Fraser

W04-193-eng-1833

Lessor: Mrs. Burton Andrews

W04-193-eng-815

Lessor: A.W. and P.D. Rosenkrans

W04-193-eng-3207 (License)

Lessor: County of Sacramento

W04-193-eng-3208 (License)

Lessor: County of Sacramento

W04-193-eng-3563 (License)

Lessor: Central Pacific and Southern Pacific Railroads

W04-193-eng-989 (Easement)

Lessor: County of Sacramento

APPENDIX B: Units at Camp Kohler

Included are some of the numbered Army Signal Corps and Army Air Forces units stationed at Camp Kohler during its short history and the WWII campaign streamers that these units earned. (Streamers in parentheses)

1st through 5th Signal Training Battalions (Western Signal Corps Training Center)

1st and 5th Signal Training Battalions (Western Signal Corps School, Davis)

274th Signal Heavy Construction Co (Leyte, Luzon, New Guinea, Southern Philippines)

276th Signal Heavy Construction Company (Leyte, Luzon, New Guinea)

359th Army Service Forces Band

840th Signal Training Bn (Moved from Camp Crowder, MO minus personnel & equipment)

983d Signal Service Company

986th Signal Service Company (Leyte, New Guinea)

1051st Overseas Replacement Depot, Camp Kohler

1081st Army Air Forces Base Unit (Overseas Replacement Depot)

1933d Station Complement Unit (SCU)

3139th Signal Motor Messenger Company (Rhineland)

3169th Signal Service Battalion (Leyte, Luzon, New Guinea)

3181st Signal Service Battalion (Okinawa) (Later became the 11th Signal Battalion)

3187th Signal Service Battalion (Central Europe, Rhineland)

3968th Service Command Unit (Stockton Ordnance Depot)

APPENDIX C: Key Military and Leadership Positions

Includes key military and civilian leadership positions at Camp Walerga; Camp Kohler; Western Signal Corps School, Davis; Camp Kohler AAF Overseas Replacement Depot; Camp Kohler Sub-Post of Camp Stoneman; and Walerga Sub-Depot, Corps of Engineers

Dates are written mm/dd/yyyy

Camp Kohler Commanding Officers

Arrival	Departure	Next Assignment

BG. Stephen H. Sherrill

| 1/1/1942 | 3/11/1943 | Fort Monmouth, NJ |

Col. Roland W. McNamee, (Acting)

| 3/11/1943 | 4/5/1943 | Drew AAF, FL |

Col. Harry E. Storms, SC

| 4/5/1943 | 6/10/44 | Fort Monmouth, NJ |

Col. James W. Green, Jr., SC

| 6/15/1944 | 8/14/1944 | Overseas |

Col. John L. Autrey, SC

| 8/15/1944 | 9/7/1944 | Camp Crowder, MO |

Col. Hugh Mitchell, SC

| 9/7/1844 | 10/31/1944 | Fort Monmouth, NJ |

Camp Kohler Garrison Command, 1933 Station Complement Unit

Col. John R. Young, FA

| 9/1/1942 | Unknown | Unknown |

Commanding Officers

	Arrival	Departure	Next Assignment

Western Signal Corps School, Davis, California

Col. Edward R. Allen, SC

	1/1943	3/5/1944	Cp. Campbell, KY

LtC. James H. Ferrick, SC (Acting)

	3/10/1944	10/31/1944	Unknown

Camp Kohler, AAF Overseas Replacement Depot

Maj. Clarence R. Case (Acting)

	12/16/1944	1/3/1945	Camp Kohler, CA

Maj. (later LtC.) Gilson A. McNeill

	1/3/1945	12/24/1945	Kearns, UT

Maj. Nels O. Olsen (Acting)

	12/24/45	2/5/1946	Kearns, UT

Camp Kohler Sub-Post of Camp Stoneman, CA, San Francisco Port of Embarkation

Col. Harry J. Farner, TC

	12/19/1945	5/5/1946	Camp Stoneman, CA

Walerga Sub-Depot, Corps of Engineers

Capt. Virgil S. Wade, CE

	1947	Unknown	Unknown

Civilian Leadership of the Sacramento Assembly Center/Camp Walerga (6 May - 26 June 1942)

Mr. Roy C. Donnally
Manager, Sacramento Office
United States Employment Service

> Mr. Donnally and his staff were responsible for registering and evacuation of Japanese Americans from the Sacramento and San Joaquin Counties to Camp Walerga.

Mr. Gene Kenyon
District Manager
Works Projects Administration (WPA)

> Mr. Kenyon and his staff were responsible for the camp administration during the period 6 May through 24 June 1942, at Camp Walerga through the Japanese American transfer to the WRA Relocation Center at Tule Lake, Modoc County, California.

APPENDIX D: War Department Inventory of Owned, Sponsored and Leased Facilities.

Includes Camp Kohler, Army Air Forces Overseas Replacement Depot, Sacramento, California. Prepared by Office of Chief of Engineers, Washington, DC, as of 31 December 1945.

- Capacity:
  - Enlisted:
    - Permanent: None
    - Mobilization: None
    - Theater of Operations (T/O): 8,602 (Billets) (T/O is type of barracks)
    - Hutments: None
    - Tents: None
    - Total: 8,602 (Billets)
  - Officers: 337 Quarters
  - Station Hospital: 334 Beds
- Acreage:
  - Owned: 3 acres
  - Leases: 3,608 acres (17 lessors)
  - Total: 3,611 acres
- Storage:
  - Covered: 120,441 square feet
  - Open: None
- Cost to Government Since 1 July 1940:
  - Annual lease payments: $11,415.00
  - Land: $219.00
  - Construction: $1,813,359.00
  - Total (less annual leases): $1,813,578.00
- Remarks."[122]

APPENDIX E: Acronyms and Abbreviations

1Lt.	First Lieutenant
1Sgt.	First Sergeant
AAF	Army Air Forces
AEF	American Expeditionary Forces
AFB	Air Force Base
AGF	Army Ground Forces
ASF	Army Service Forces
AVG	American Volunteer Group
BG.	Brigadier General
CA	California
Capt.	Captain
CE	Corps of Engineers
CNAC	China National Aviation Corporation
Col.	Colonel
CP	Camp
Cpl.	Corporal
DC	District of Columbia
DENSHO	To Pass on to the Next Generation of Japanese
DoD	Department of Defense
ESCRTC	Eastern Signal Corps Training Center
ESCUTC	Eastern Signal Corps Unit Training Center
FA	Field Artillery

FBI	Federal Bureau of Investigation
GI	Government Issue
HQ	Headquarters
JACL	Japanese American Citizens League
LtG.	Lieutenant General
LtC.	Lieutenant Colonel
Maj.	Major
MG.	Major General
mm	Millimeter
Pvt.	Private
PW	Prisoner of War
RKO	Radio-Keith Orpheum
SC	Signal Corps
SCU	Service Command Unit
SF	San Francisco
SGM	Sergeant Major
SoS	Services of Supply
T/O	Theater of Operations
TC	Transportation Corps
USO	United Services Organization
VFW	Veterans of Foreign Wars
WCCA	Wartime Civil Control Administration
WPA	Works Projects Administration
WRA	War Relocation Authority

WSCRTC	Western Signal Corps Replacement Training Center
WSCS	Western Signal Corps School
WSCUTC	Western Signal Corps Unit Training Center
WWI	World War I
WWII	World War II

APPENDIX F: Annotated Camp Kohler Layout Map

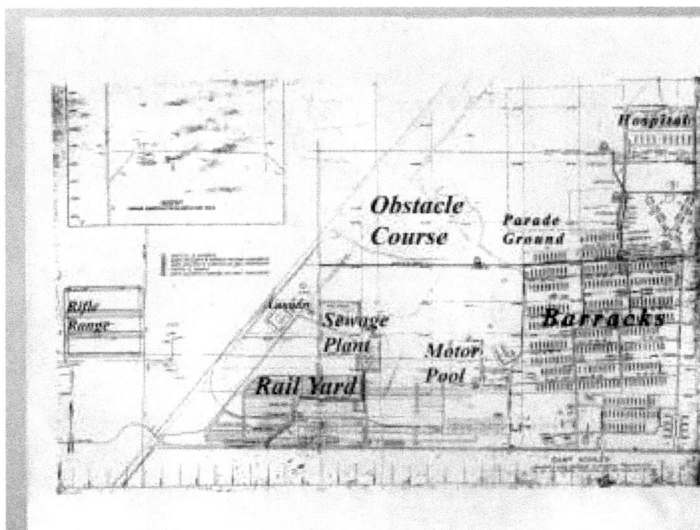

Camp Kohler Formerly Used Defense Site No. J09CA7063. Annotated by Beverly Johnson

1 DeWitt, J. L. (1943). *Final Report, Japanese Evacuation from the West Coast 1942,* Washington, DC: GPO. The official War Relocation Authority definition of Assembly Center is "[A] temporary enclosed area maintained by [the] Army where persons of Japanese ancestry were housed and fed during [the] primary stages of evacuation prior to transfer to War Relocation Projects."

2 De Witt., p. 151. The Sacramento Assembly Center was built new from the ground up unlike other centers   converted from racetracks and fairgrounds.

3 DeWitt Inspects Nearby Japanese Assembly Center. (1942, May 2). *Sacramento Bee,* p. 21. Retrieved December 16, 2015, from http://infoweb.newsbank.com/resources/doc/nb/image/v2:144FDEA786229ACC@EANX-NB-14F905DBDED24AE1@2430482-14F8F755E808FDC0@20-4F93EFF9B5285A8@?p=AMNEWS

4 Burton, J., Farrell, M., Lord, F., & Lord, R. (2000). *Confinement and Ethnicity: An Overview of World War II Japanese American Relocation Sites* (Chapter 16). Washington, DC: National Park Service. Retrieved August 20, 2016 from https://www.nps.gov/parkhistory/online books/anthropology74/ce16i.htm.

5 Report of the American Red Cross Survey of Assembly Centers in California, Oregon, and Washington. [microform]. (n.d.). *In Papers of the U.S. Commission on Wartime Relocation and Internment of Civilians, Part 1.* Numerical file archive. Reel 10. Retrieved September 2016 from http://www.lib.washington.edu/exhibits/harmony/Exhibit/layout.html
In practically all the centers, the families are housed in newly constructed Theatre of Operations [T/O] type of barracks buildings which are constructed according to the following general specifications: size 20 x 100 ft.

built directly on the ground or supported by wooden blocks for foundation; and with 2 x 4 floor joist installed for wooden floors. In many centers, some of the barracks buildings have concrete or asphalt floors. The sidewalls are made of horizontal one-inch boards, except for the Puyallup Center [Washington], and covered with 30 lb. felt or one-ply roofing paper. Roof is simple gable with 2 x 4 rafters on 2 to 8 ft. centers covered with one-inch boards to which one layer of one-ply roofing has been applied. These buildings are divided into rooms or apartments with wooden partition walls extending from the floor to the top of the outside wall line, leaving open a space above the ceiling joist to the roof. Each apartment in the T.O. type of buildings has one door and two or more windows. Except for one or two centers, all windows are screened and in some instances screen doors have been supplied.

[6] Magagnini, S. (2015, Aug 26). Detention center plaque rededicated -Granite plaque labeled 'Lest We Forget' honors Japanese Americans incarcerated during WWII. Earlier plaque vandalized before Sacramento County financed refurbishing of the site. Japanese Americans, many of them citizens, were forced to leave behind homes and possessions. *Sacramento Bee,* p.3A. Retrieved February 4, 2017 from http://infoweb.newsbank.com/resources/doc/nb/news/157943CA4A545538?p=AMNEWS

[7] Movement of Japanese Is Started Here. (1942, May 13) *Sacramento Bee*, p.13. Retrieved June 18, 2016, from http://infoweb.newsbank.com/resources/doc/nb/image/v2:144FDEA786229ACC@EANX-NB-14F905E136332292@2430493-14F903022893BCAB@0?p=AMNEWS

8 All Japanese Must Get Out of Sacramento. (1942, May 7).
    Sacramento Bee, pp.1-14. Retrieved May 24, 2016, from
    http://infoweb.newsbank.com/resources/doc/nb/image
    /v2:144FDEA786229ACC@EANX-NB-
    14F905DE84F8C9DB@2430487-14F8F7DC4AE558C3@0-
    4F93DE4FB42E600@?p=AMNEWS
9Japanese Hope Reception Camp Will End Worries. (1942, May
    8). *Sacramento Bee*, p.18. Retrieved March 14, 2016
    from
    http://infoweb.newsbank.com/resources/doc/nb/image
    /v2:144FDEA786229ACC@EANX-NB-
    14F905DF02B8AC27@2430488-
    14F8AE7AA9F64123@17?p=AMNEWS
10 De Witt. p.231.
11 Japanese Are Being Moved from Walerga. (1942, June
    15). *Sacramento Bee*, p. 18. Retrieved September 10,
    2016, from
    http://infoweb.newsbank.com/resources/doc/nb/image
    /v2:144FDEA786229ACC@EANX-NB-
    4FA3A5EA2D88533@2430526-14F8AE713613DAE6@17-
    14FA4BB6AB657F40@?p=AMNEWS
12 Officials Say Walerga Will Be Used for Other Purposes. (1942,
    June 20). *Sacramento Bee*, p. 2. Retrieved May 21, 2016,
    from
    http://infoweb.newsbank.com/resources/doc/nb/image
    /v2:144FDEA786229ACC@EANX-NB-
    14FA3A60960722C0@2430531-
    14F8AE7308E833F7@1?p=AMNEWS
13 Ibid.
14 De Witt. pp.346, 349.
15 Terrett, D. Thompson, G., Harris, D. R., & Oakes, P. M. (1957).
    *The Signal Corps: The Test: December 1941 to July
    1943*. Washington, DC: Center of Military History p. 196.
16 Ibid. p. 197

[17] An SCU is a unit that by design is a support unit that is responsible for facilities necessary for support of Army activities on post including messing, billeting, mail, maintenance, and security.

[18] Signal Training Unit Will Open on Walerga Site. (1942, August 20) *Sacramento Bee*, p. 1. Retrieved December 5, 2015, from http://infoweb.newsbank.com/resources/doc/nb/image/v2:144FDEA786229ACC@EANX-NB

[19] Sherrill to Head California Post. (1942, August 22). *Ashbury Park Press*, p. 1. Retrieved September 20, 2016, from https://www.newspapers.com/image/14421268.

[20] *The Crash of CNAC's Last DC-2, The Accident – March 14, 1942*. Retrieved 7/29/2016, from http://cnac.org/emilscott/accid01.htm.

[21] Kohler Named After Signal Officer Killed in China. (1942, November 26). *The Western Signal Corps Message*, Camp Kohler, CA., pp. 1,4.

[22] *Kohler, Frederick Lincoln, 1st LT US Army*. US Department of Veterans Affairs, National Cemetery Administration, Nationwide Gravesite Locator. Retrieved July 29, 2016, from http://gravelocator.cem.va.gov/index.html?cemetery=N895.

[23] Terrett. p. 197

[24] Darmstad, M. (1987, April 23). Once a Joke, Now a Memory. Camp Kohler Trainees Gather to Celebrate Four Decades Later. *Sacramento Bee*, p. B6. Retrieved December 25, 2016, from http://infoweb.newsbank.com/resources/doc/nb/news/0EB0D7B6EFA3717A?p=AMNEWS.

[25] *Historic California Posts, Camps and Stations, Camp Kohler (Sacramento Assembly Center, Walerga Engineer Depot, and Prisoner of War Branch Camp)*. (2015, December 2). California State Military Museum. Retrieved October 24, 2016 from http://militarymuseum.org/CpKohler.html. p.5.

[26] Ibid.

[27] Ibid.

[28] Ibid.

[29] Terrett. p. 319.

[30] Training Will Begin This Week at Camp Kohler. (1942, September 15). *Sacramento Bee*, p. 5. Retrieved December 24, 2016, from http://infoweb.newsbank.com/resources/doc/nb/image/v2:144FDEA786229ACC@EANX-NB-14FA44DE74CF3F3D@2430618-14FA3CE331DBD019@4?p=AMNEWS.

[31] Ibid.

[32] Terrett. p.319.

[33] War Department, (WD) GO No. 54, (1942, Oct. 14), Sub: Designation of Military Reservations, Camp Kohler (named in honor of 1Lt. Frederick L. Kohler, Signal Corps, U S Army).

[34] Ibid.

[35] Certain Victory is Forecast at Camp Kohler Dedication. (1942, Dec 2). *Sacramento Bee*, p. 6. Retrieved from http://infoweb.newsbank.com/resources/doc/nb/image/v2:144FDEA786229ACC@EANX-NB-14FA35060DD7DB39@2430696-14F8AA41602A3F73@5-4FA4019AFE4D188?p=AMNEWS

[36] Camp Kohler Rites Will Be Broadcast. (1942, December 2). S*acramento Bee*, p. 19. Retrieved May 23, 2016, from http://infoweb.newsbank.com/resources/doc/nb/image/v2:144FDEA786229ACC@EANX-NB-14F.

[37] Sacramentan Receives Government Contract. (1942, July 30). *Sacramento Bee*, p. 5. Retrieved March 3, 2016, from http://infoweb.newsbank.com/resources/doc/nb/image /v2:144FDEA786229ACC@EANX-NB-14FA3D80C42A9E26@2430571-14FA3D32C3E3E15D@14FA751875627930@?p=AMNEWS.

[38] Tent Theater Will Entertain Soldiers. (1942, October 20). *Sacramento Bee*, p. 31. Retrieved February 9, 2016, from http://infoweb.newsbank.com/resources/doc/nb/image /v2:144FDEA786229ACC@EANX-NB-14FA3B897AA2183A@2430653-14FA386608D6C60E@30-4FA53801C1ACB30@?p=AMNEWS.

[39] Camp Kohler's New Chapel Is to Be Dedicated. (1942, November 28). *Sacramento Bee*, p. 12. Retrieved December 5, 2015, from http://infoweb.newsbank.com/resources/doc/nb/image /v2:144FDEA786229ACC@EANX-NB-14FA4038090ACC5E@24030692-14F8AA402A93B2AD@11-14FA57336E3164C8@?p=AMNEWS.

[40] Kohler Building Work Is Speeded. (1942, December 19). *Sacramento Bee*, p. 19. Retrieved December 5, 2015, from http://infoweb.newsbank.com/resources/doc/nb/image /v2:144FDEA786229ACC@EANX-NB-14FA350E2F08C5D1@2430713-14FA3381E5CDE124@18-14FA42AAC37EAF10?p=AMNEWS.

[41] Hospital Will Move. (1942, December 10). *The Western Signal Corps Message,* Camp Kohler, CA, p. 1.

[42] Hall is Finished at Camp Kohler. (1942, November 24). *Sacramento Bee*, p. 15. Retrieved December 27, 2016, from http://infoweb.newsbank.com/resources/doc/nb/ image /v2:144FDEA786229ACC@EANX-NB-14FA4030A5A5689B@2430688-14FA3EEBC2C1634F@14?p=AMNEWS.

[43] Guest House Is Opened at Camp. (1943, January 16). *Sacramento Bee*, p. 4. Retrieved December 6, 2015, from http://infoweb.newsbank.com/resources/doc/nb/image/v2:144FDEA786229ACC@EANX-NB-14FA44DE74CF3F3D@2430618-14FA3CE331DBD019@4?p=AMNEWS.

[44] Camp Kohler Theater Gets Modern Seats. (1944, January 1). *Sacramento Bee*, p. 5. Retrieved December 27, 2016, from http://infoweb.newsbank.com/resources/doc/nb/image/v2:144FDEA786229ACC@EANX-NB-14F8F1C082359CAC@2431091-14F8EC94C2ACA7BE@44F912A1261920C8@?p=AMNEWS.

[45] *Historic California Posts, Camps, and Stations, Camp Kohler*, p. 5.

[46] Camp Kohler Streets Will Be Named for U.S. Military Heroes. (1942, October 23). *Sacramento Bee*, p. 20, Retrieved May 1, 2016, from http://infoweb.newsbank.com/resources/doc/nb/image/v2:144FDEA786229ACC@EANX-NB-14FA3B8B94B9D585@2430656-14F8AA340C05F522@19?p=AMNEWS.

[47] *Historic California Posts, Camps, and Stations, Camp Kohler*, p. 4.

[48] Camp Kohler's New Rifle Range is Opened. (1942, Nov 27). *Sacramento Bee*, p.16. Retrieved December 31, 2015 from http://infoweb.newsbank.com/resources/doc/nb/image/v2:144FDEA786229ACC@EANX-NB-14FA403505ACD722@2430691-14FA3F7FF1408629@15?p=AMNEWS.

[49] Darmstad, M. (1987, April 23).

[50] *Historic California Posts, Camps, and Stations, Camp Kohler*, p.6.

[51] Ibid.

[52] Signal Corpsmen Hold Field Exercise. (1943, May 27). *Sacramento Bee*, p. 12. Retrieved March 11, 2017 from http://infoweb.newsbank.com/resources/doc/nb/image/v2:144FDEA786229ACC@EANX-NB-14FB3F4F3AB8C1C8@2430872-14F851C54D2A8435@11-14FB61B215DAA290@?p=AMNEWS.

[53] Kohler Builds Village for Combat Training. (1943, Sep 24). *Sacramento Bee*, p. 23. Retrieved @?p=AMNEWS December 12, 2015, from http://infoweb.newsbank.com/resources/doc/nb/image/v2: 144FDEA786229ACC@EANX-NB-14F938DAE7242566@2430992-14F9378C10C1521C@22-14F94BA31CE585A0.

[54] Cargo Net Climbing Added to Post Training Program. (1943, Sep 9) *The Western Signal Corps Message,* Camp Kohler, CA, p.1.

[55] The Office of the Chief Signal Officer. *Signal Corps Technical Information Letter No.24.* (1943, November) p. 61. Washington, DC: War Department.

[56] Getting Their Sea Legs on Dry Land. (1943, Oct 30). *Sacramento Bee*, p. 24. Retrieved January 30, 2017 from http://infoweb.newsbank.com/resources/doc/nb/image/v2:144FDEA786229ACC@EANX-NB-14FA995EA149C909@2431028-14F851FD04E862A2@23-14FAE19087473090@?p=AMNEWS

[57] The Office of the Chief Signal Officer. (1943, November). p. 63.

[58] Camp Swimming Pool Was Bought by GIs. (1944, September 14) *The Western Signal Corps Message, Camp* Kohler, CA, p.11.

[59] Movie Actors to Entertain Saturday. (1943, April 15). *The Western Signal Corps Message,* Camp Kohler, CA, p. 1.

[60] Ibid.

[61] Prop Man Swartz Did Movie Miracles. (1943, May 27). *The Western Signal Corps Message,* Camp Kohler, CA, p. 3.

[62] Faith Cathcart Wins Camp Beauty Contest. (1943, June 9), *Sacramento Bee*, p. 14. Retrieved October 19, 2016 from http://infoweb.newsbank.com/resources/doc/nb/image /v2:144FDEA786229ACC@EANX-NB-14F8E13BC4378A3C@2430885-14F851CCF463532B@13?p=AMNEWS.

[63] Soldiers Reach Town through Convoy System. (1942, October 16). *Sacramento Bee*, p. 2. Retrieved May 1, 2016, from http://infoweb.newsbank.com/resources/doc/nb/image /v2:144FDEA786229ACC@EANX-NB-14FA3B8747137922@2430649-14F8AA3180D72FDE@1?p=AMNEWS.

[64] 500 Soldiers Volunteer. (1942, September 25). *Sacramento Bee*, p. 19. Retrieved February 9, 2016, from http://infoweb.newsbank.com/resources/doc/nb/image /v2:144FDEA786229ACC@EANX-NB-14FA44E5CA3601D8@2430628-14FA42E2D7396E82@18-14FA5ABAE6B7C9F8@?p=AMNEWS.

[65] Davis Soldiers Will Help in Canneries. (1943, Aug 13). *Sacramento Bee*, p. 11. Retrieved October 3, 2016 from http://infoweb.newsbank.com/resources/doc/nb/image /v2:144FDEA786229ACC@EANX-NB-14F8ED0537D3BB32@2430950-14F8EAA3E34BDEE2@10-14F9254A85599D18@?p=AMNEWS.

[66] The Office of the Chief Signal Officer. *Signal Corps Technical Information Letter No.14, (1943, January)*. Washington, DC: War Department. pp. 6-7.

[67] *Historical Data - Post, Camp, Station or Air Field, Western Signal Corps School, (California Agriculture College), Davis, California.* Retrieved from http://www.militarymuseum.org/Davis.html p.1.

[68] Signal Corps Takes Over at Davis College. (1943, Feb 3). *Sacramento Bee*, p. 6. Retrieved September 30, 2016 from http://infoweb.newsbank.com/resources/doc/nb/image/v2:144FDEA786229ACC@EANX-NB-14FA40ED02628D72@2430759-14F8AA54A0A22E98@5-14FA581467DDBFE0@?p=AMNEWS.

[69] Ibid.

[70] Cannon Sounds Davis Reveille. (1943, Mar 26). *Sacramento Bee*, p. 8. Retrieved December 5, 2015 from http://infoweb.newsbank.com/resources/doc/nb/image/v2:144FDEA786229ACC@EANX-NB-14FB01A4ABB417F5@2430810-14F8AA6499EC5B00@7-14FB162A9BEDA0B0@?p=AMNEWS.

[71] Keene, L. (2013, November 6). Yolo at war: Signal Corps took over on Davis Campus. *The Davis Enterprise*, Davis, CA. Retrieved August 21, 2017, from http://www.davisenterprise.com/local-news/with-students-faculty-at-war-davis-campus-trained-signal-corps-soldiers/

[72] Army Changes Davis Names. (1943, Mar 11). *Sacramento Bee*, p. 8. Retrieved June 22, 2016 from http://infoweb.newsbank.com/resources/doc/nb/image/v2:144FDEA786229ACC@EANX-NB-14FB019A6D3078E9@2430795-14F8AA60166115D1@7-14FB15B9D0CC04B0@?p=AMNEWS.

[73] Thompson, G.R. & Harris, D. R. (1991). *United States Army in World War II, The Technical Services, The Signal Corps. The Outcome (Mid-1943 Through 1945.* Washington DC. Center of Military History, United States Army. p.517.

[74] Kohler Commander Reorganizes Camp. (1944, January 6). *Nevada State Journal, Reno, NV*, p. 8. Retrieved August 19, 2016, from https://www.newspapers.com/image/75299045.

[75] Thompson. p. 518.

[76] Ibid. p.523

[77] Ibid.

[78] Kohler Will Start Desk Men to Combat. (1944, Feb 21). *Sacramento Bee,* p. 6. Retrieved June 24, 2016 from http://infoweb.newsbank.com/resources/doc/nb/image/v2:144FDEA786229ACC@EANX-NB-14FB44E29C887439@2431142-14F858E4006D46FD@5?p=AMNEWS.

[79] Camp Kohler Goes on Nine Hour Day. (1944, Aug 10). *Sacramento Bee,* p. 3. Retrieved January 26, 2017 from http://infoweb.newsbank.com/resources/doc/nb/image/v2:144FDEA786229ACC@EANX-NB-14FF29048FC34153@2431313-14FF24EC9E5F7A72@2?p=AMNEWS.

[80] Camp Hospital Sets Outstanding Record. (1944, Sep 14). *Western Signal Corps Message.* Camp Kohler, CA, p.1.

[81] Camp Kohler Paper Is Issued for Last Time. (1944, Sep 15). *Sacramento Bee,* p. 15. Retrieved December 6, 2015 from http://infoweb.newsbank.com/resources/doc/nb/image/v2:144FDEA786229ACC@EANX-NB-14FB47204CC9765B@2431349-14FB45128ECD6831@14?p=AMNEWS.

[82] Col. H.E. Storms Takes Command. (1943, Apr 5). *Sacramento Bee,* p.1. Retrieved December 6, 2015 from http://infoweb.newsbank.com/resources/doc/nb/image/v2:144FDEA786229ACC@EANX-NB-14F8E6AB143455A8@2430820-14F8E2D7509068C0@0?p=AMNEWS.

[83] Storms Gets Reeder's Post. (1944, Jun 15). Ashbury Park Press, Asbury Park, NJ. p.1. Retrieved August 28, 2016 from https://www.newspapers.com/images/143454527.

[84] Camp Murphy Loses Founder to Calif. (1944, Jun 15). *The Palm Beach Post*, p.6. Retrieved August 28, 2016 from https://www.newspapers.com/images/133686816.

[85] New Commander of Kohler Assumes Post. (1944, Aug 16). *Sacramento Bee*, p. 4. Retrieved June 23, 2016 from http://infoweb.newsbank.com/resources/doc/nb/image /v2:144FDEA786229ACC@EANX-NB-14FF29089B4AD475@2431319-14FEEEB99587CF53@3-14FF30DCB2BEEBC8@?p=AMNEWS.

[86] Col. Mitchell Takes Command at Kohler. (1944, Sep 7). *Sacramento Bee*, p. 1. Retrieved December 6, 2015 from http://infoweb.newsbank.com/resources/doc/nb/image /v2:144FDEA786229ACC@EANX-NB-imageimages/114FB471B578CF671@2431341-14FB43CF93714C67@0-14FB73B955240C60@?13366p=AMNEWS.

[87] Colonel Is Honored. (1944, Mar 10). *Sacramento Bee*, p. 43. Retrieved July 13, 2016 from http://infoweb.newsbank.com/resources/doc/nb/image /v2:144FDEA786229ACC@EANX-NB-4FC8215ED2C2C57@2431160-14FB4DE105177116@42-14FCA0B67A7C1390@?p=AMNEWS.

[88] Camp Kohler Will Be Kept on Active Basis. (1944, Oct 24). *Sacramento Bee*, p. 1. Retrieved February 5, 2017 from http://infoweb.newsbank.com/resources/doc/nb/image /v2:144FDEA786229ACC@EANX-NB-14FC81014D36E697@2431388-14FC7FBD5113BD1A@0?p=AMNEWS.

[89] Kohler Officials Await Orders on Camp Transfer. (1944, Nov 1).*Sacramento Bee*, p. 5. Retrieved June 24, 2016 from http://infoweb.newsbank.com/resources/doc/nb/image /v2:144FDEA786229ACC@EANX-NB14FC85162215FF0Drces@2431396-14FC81A8CDAC95E5@4-14FCACC55C22DD98@?p=AMNEWS.

[90] ROTC Will Arrive at Camp Tomorrow. (1945, Mar 23).
Sacramento Bee, p. 4. Retrieved October 21, 2016 from
http://infoweb.newsbank.com/resources/doc/nb/image
/v2:144FDEA786229ACC@EANX-NB-
14FB8FC08EF87684@2431538-14FA9E5B1367340A@3-
14FBA5947A987530@?p=AMNEWS

[91] Kohler Becomes Replacement Site for Air Forces. (1944, Dec
16). *Sacramento Bee*, p. 7. Retrieved December 6, 2015
from
http://infoweb.newsbank.com/resources/doc/nb/image
/v2:144FDEA786229ACC@EANX-NB-
4FC8A0BB01CD140@2431441-14FC8825F2FA97D9@6-
14FCD631AE291BB0@?p=AMNEWS.

[92] Alert Boys Help to Capture Escaped PW. (1945, Jul
17). *Sacramento Bee*, p. 2. Retrieved December 20, 2015
from
http://infoweb.newsbank.com/resources/doc/nb/image
/v2:144FDEA786229ACC@EANX-
NB14FC81AAC57D55B4@2431654-
14FAA4B7A819FAF6@1-
14FC9F967072D8E8@?p=AMNEWS.

[93] Reclassification of Installation. (1946, Jan 5) *Circular #4*, War
Department, Washington DC: AGO 680.1. Section III, p.2.

[94] *Historical Data - Post, Camp, Station, or Air Field: Walerga
Sub-Depot.* p.11. Retrieved December 1, 2016 from
http://militarymuseum.org/CpKohler.html.

[95] Engineers Will Take Over Camp Kohler. (1946, Mar 19).
Sacramento Bee, p. 1. Retrieved October 22, 2016 from
http://infoweb.newsbank.com/resources/doc/nb/image
/v2:144FDEA786229ACC@EANX-NB-
144FF4E66CF552FD@2431899-
144FF395A951DF76@0?p=AMNEWS.

[96] Sacramento Protests. (1945, Nov 4). *The San Bernardino
County Sun,* p. 1. Retrieved July 12, 2016
from https://www.newspapers.com/images/49373837.

[97] VFW Protests Camp Use by Japanese. (1945, Nov 10). *Sacramento Bee, p.1.* Retrieved October 22, 2016 from http://infoweb.newsbank.com/resources/doc/nb/o,age/v2:144FDEA78229ACC@EANX-NB-14FC84760FEB15@2431770-14FAA5693470ABDE@3?P=AMNEWS.

[98] *Historical Data - Post, Camp, Station or Air Field, Camp Kohler, Walerga Sub-Depot, p.11*

[99] Ibid., p6.

[100] Ibid., p11.

[101] Bribery Gets Local Man 18 Month Term. (1947, Apr 14) *Sacramento Bee, p.1.* Retrieved September 4, 2016 from http://infoweb.newsbank.com/resources/doc/nb/image/v2:144FDEA78622ACC@EANX-NB145092A3425CDF032432290-1450901FD0348865@0?P=AMNEWS

[102] Trial of Bribery, Theft Charges Is Under Way. (1947, Mar 26). *Sacramento Bee, p.16.* Retrieved September 4, 2016 from http://infoweb.newsbank.com/resources/doc/nb/image/v2:144FDEA786229ACC@EANX-NB-1450D0084E3C06B2@2432274-1450845CAEB4C734@15?P=AMNEWS

[103] More Fireman Are Needed; Lloyd Ervine. (1947, Jul 3). *Sacramento Bee, p. 18.* Retrieved February 5, 2017 from http://infoweb.newsbank.com/resources/doc/nb/image/v2:144FDEA786229ACC@EANX-NB-14502CC8978678D9@2432370-1450212F1569FC17@17?p=AMNEWS

[104] Flames Wipe Out 50 Buildings at California Camp; (1947, June 21). *The Waco News-Tribune, p. 1.* Retrieved July 7, 2016 from https://www.newspapers.com/image/47952063/?terms=Flames%2BWipe%2BOut%2B50%2BBuildings%2BAt%2BCalifornia%2BCamp.

[105] Fire Levels Half of Camp Kohler, Sweeps Homes; Reed Jordan; (1947, Jun 21). *Sacramento Bee*, p. 1. Retrieved July 7, 2016 from http://infoweb.newsbank.com/resources/doc/nb/image/v2:144FDEA786229ACC@EANX-NB-145027A851F74A59@2432358-14502132F8189E48@0?p=AMNEWS.

[106] Nearly All Buildings at Kohler Are Sold. (1947, Oct 14). *Sacramento Bee*, p. 25. Retrieved February 4, 2017 from http://infoweb.newsbank.com/resources/doc/nb/image/v2:144FDEA786229ACC@EANX-NB-145040BCAD1E827D@2432473-14502B9DCE43EA25@24?p=AMNEWS.

[107] Veterans Purchase 37 War Surplus Kohler Buildings. (1948, Dec 6). *Sacramento Bee*, p. 29. Retrieved October 7, 2016 from http://infoweb.newsbank.com/resources/doc/nb/image/v2:144FDEA786229ACC@EANX-NB-14508936DBBAB969@2432892-14507CA5F0B81D9C@28-1450BD912EA350D8@?p=AMNEWS.

[108] Camp Kohler Is to Be Used by National Guard. (1948, Nov 8). *Sacramento Bee*, p. 2. Retrieved July 7, 2016 from http://infoweb.newsbank.com/resources/doc/nb/image/v2:144FDEA786229ACC@EANX-NB-14508F174C45060D@2432864-14507CB0208957B0@1-1450C6287AAB0718@?p=AMNEWS.

[109] Church Buys Kohler Chapel for Mission. (1949, Jan 25). *Sacramento Bee*, p. 8. Retrieved on June 25, 2016 from http://infoweb.newsbank.com/resources/doc/nb/image/v2:144FDEA786229ACC@EANX-NB-1450CD1AD364E451@2432942-14508FDEE976A375@7?p=AMNEWS.

[110] Site Obtained for Citrus Heights Chapel. (1949, Mar 11). *Sacramento Bee*, p. 8. Retrieved on March 5, 2016 from http://infoweb.newsbank.com/resources/doc/nb/image /v2:144FDEA786229ACC@EANX-NB-1450D35FCAE19DB2@2432987-14508FE7B52C1742@7?p=AMNEWS.

[111] Camp Kohler May Reopen for Training. (1951, Jan 18). *Sacramento Bee*, p. 1. Retrieved December 9, 2015 from http://infoweb.newsbank.com/resources/doc/nb/image /v2:144FDEA786229ACC@EANX-NB-14FAF309E8A4DF57@2433665-14F8BBAF226D5530@0-14FB1B4CB9C07068@?p=AMNEWS.

[112] $64,261,999 Is Urged for Camp Kohler. (1951, Jan 26). *Sacramento Bee*, p. 1. Retrieved December 11, 2015 from http://infoweb.newsbank.com/resources/doc/nb/image /v2:144FDEA786229ACC@EANX-NB-14FAF310791A9DF6@2433673-14F8BBBF214EB5FB@0?p=AMNEWS.

[113] Ibid.

[114] Air Force Abandons Plan to Use Kohler. (1951, Apr 25). *Sacramento Bee*, p. 1. Retrieved December 9, 2015 from http://infoweb.newsbank.com/resources/doc/nb/image /v2:144FDEA786229ACC@EANX-NB-14FB37C167D2C318@2433762-14FA362CDE19D8A6@0-14FB56C70C7E7C80@?p=AMNEWS.

[115] Developer Plans $100 Million Community in North Suburbs. (1958, Dec 1). *Sacramento Bee*, p. 1. Retrieved from http://infoweb.newsbank.com/resources/doc/nb/image /v2:144FDEA786229ACC@EANX-NB-14FCEF87802C3425@2436539-14FAB51A275D7097@0-14FD2FBEC30360A8?p=AMNEWS.

[116] Ike Signs Bill Giving County Sewage Plant. (1959, Sep 23). *Sacramento Bee*, p. 15. Retrieved July 12, 2016 from http://infoweb.newsbank.com/resources/doc/nb/image /v2:144FDEA786229ACC@EANX-NB-

14FCDE34BB895ED2@2436835-
14FB2F12A02B4B88@14-
14FD0E9ED9B83E68@?p=AMNEWS.

[117] Ibid.

[118] Magagnini, S. (2015, Aug 26). Detention center plaque rededicated, p.3A.

[119] *Historic California Posts, Camps and Stations, Camp Kohler.* p.6.

[120] Gilmore, R. (1984, November 30). Landmark Goes Down. *Sacramento Bee*, p. B01. Retrieved August 15, 2016 from http://infoweb.newsbank.com/resources/doc/nb/news/0EB0D5B3C4D86446?p=AMNEWS.

[121] Request for Authorization of Project 330 Funds for Guarding and Maintenance of Camp Kohler. (1946, Apr 17) *Board Report, Section II, Real Property. General Description,* p.2. Sacramento, CA: Army Service Forces, Corps of Engineers, Office of the District Engineer, Sacramento District.

[122] *War Department Inventory of Owned, Sponsored, and Leased Facilities: Camp Kohler, Army Air Forces Overseas Replacement Depot, Sacramento, California* (1945, Dec 31). Washington, D.C: Office of Chief of Engineers, *p.51.*

BIBLIOGRAPHY

Aerial view of Sacramento Assembly Center, California, c. 1942. (2015, July 17). In *Densho Encyclopedia*. Retrieved, March 27, 2018 from https://encyclopedia.densho.org/sources/en-denshopd-i224-00009-1/

Asbury Park Press, (August 22,1942-June 15,1944). Asbury Park. NJ, Retrieved from https://www.newspapers.com/images/143454527

Burton, J., Farrell, M., Lord, F., & Lord, R. (2000, September 1). *An Overview of World War II Japanese American Relocation Sites*. Retrieved from https://www.nps.gov/parkhistory/online_books/anthropology74/

Department of Veterans Affairs, (2016, July 29). Kohler, Frederick Lincoln, 1st LT US Army, buried at Golden Gate National Cemetery, burial site N895. Retrieved from https://gravelocator.cem.va.gov/

DeWitt, J. L. (1943). *Final Report: Japanese Evacuation from the West Coast*. 1942. Washington, DC: Government Printing Office.

General Order No. 54, Subject: Designations of Military Reservations, Camp Kohler (named in honor of 1Lt. Frederick L. Kohler, Signal Corps, US Army). (1942, October 14). Washington, DC: War Department.

Historic California Post, Camps and Stations, Camp Kohler (Sacramento Assembly Center, Walerga Engineer Depot, and Prisoner of War Branch Camp). (2015, October 2). Retrieved October 24, 2016, from http://militarymuseum.org/CpKohler.html

Historic California Posts, Camps, Stations and Airfields, Western Signal Corps School, Davis (University of California College of Agriculture). (2015, March 1). Retrieved March 25, 2018, from https://www.militarymuseum.org/Davis.html

Historic California Posts: Camp Kohler (Sacramento Assembly Center, Walerga Engineer Depot, and Prisoner War Branch Camp). (2015, December 2). Retrieved from http://www.militarymuseum.org/CpKohler.html

Johnson, D. M. (2017). Camp Kohler, California. *On Point, The Journal of Army History*, Army Historical Foundation, 22(3), 46-49.

Keene, L. (2013, November 6). Yolo at war: Signal Corps took over on Davis Campus. *The Davis Enterprise*, p. 13. Retrieved from http://www.davisenterprise.com/local-news/with-students-faculty-at-war-davis-campus-trained-signal-corps-soldiers/

Kohler Commander Reorganizes Camp. (1944, January 6). *Nevada State Journal*, p. 8. Retrieved from http://www.newspapers.com/image/75299045

Lange, Dorothea [photographer]. (May 20, 1942) A newly arrived family at the Sacramento Assembly Center, California. Reprinted (2015, July 17).in *Densho Encyclopedia*. Retrieved, March 27, 2018 from https://encyclopedia.densho.org/sources/en-denshopd-i151-00027-1/

Office of the Adjutant General. (1946). *Reclassification of Installation Circular No.4 (p. 2)*. Washington, DC: War Department.

Office of the Chief Signal Officer. (1943). *Signal Corps Technical Information Letter No.14* (pp. 6-7). Washington, DC: War Department.

Office of the Chief Signal Officer. (1943). *Signal Corps Technical Information Letter No.24* (p. 61). Washington, DC: War Department.

Report of the American Red Cross Survey of Assembly Centers in California, Oregon, and Washington. *Papers of the U.S. Commission on Wartime Relocation and Internment of Civilians. Part 1*. Retrieved from http://www.lib.washington.edu/exhibits/harmony/Exhibit/layout.html

Roberts, R. B. (1988). *Encyclopedia of Historic Forts: The Military, Pioneer, and Trading Posts of the United States*. New York, NY: MacMillan Publishing Company.

Radio News, Special U.S. Army Signal Corps Issue, (February 1944). 31(2), 98-113.

Sacramento Bee, 8 February 1942 – July 2010.

Sacramento Protests. (1945, November 4). *The San Bernardino County Sun*, p. 1. Retrieved from https://newspapers.com/images/49373837

Scheuring, A. F. (2001). *Abundant Harvest: The History of the University of California, Davis*. Davis, CA: UC Davis History Project.

Terrett, D., Thompson, G., Harris, D., & Oakes, P. (1957). *THE SIGNAL CORPS: The Test* (December 1941 to July 1943). Washington, DC: Center of Military History.

The Crash of CNAC's Last DC-2. (2016 July 29). Retrieved from http://cnac.org/emilscott/accid01.htm

The Palm Beach Post (1944, June 15). Retrieved from https://www.newspapers.com/images/133686816

The Waco News-Tribune, (1947, June 21) Retrieved from https://www.newspapers.com/images/47952063

The Western Signal Corps Message, (Nov 1942-Sep 1944), Camp Kohler, CA.

Thompson, G. R., & Harris, D. R. (1966). *THE SIGNAL CORPS: The Outcome* (Mid-1943 through 1945). Washington, DC: Center of Military History.

UC Davis Quad [Photograph]. (1944). Larkey Collection, Yolo County Archives, Woodland, CA.

Various Photographic Images. (1943). *A Camera Trip Through Camp Kohler*. Brooklyn, New York: The Ullman Co.

Various Photographic Images. (1942-1944). *Radio News. Special U.S. Army Signal Corps Issue.*

Various Photographic Images. (1942-1944). *The Western Signal Corps Message*, Camp Kohler, Sacramento and the Western Signal Corps School, Davis, California. B. J. Johnson (Compiler).

War Department Inventory of Owned, Sponsored, and Leased Facilities: Camp Kohler, Army Air Forces Overseas Replacement Depot, Sacramento, CA. (1945, December 31). Washington, DC: Office of Chief of Engineers.

Wise, N. E., MAJ. (1946, April 17*). Request for Authorization of Project 330 Funds for Guarding and Maintenance of Camp Kohler* [Letter to The Division Engineer, South Pacific Division, San Francisco, CA]. Corps of Engineers, Office of the District Engineer, Sacramento, California.